THE VIEW FROM GOAK HILL

A CHRISTIAN'S PERSPECTIVE ON LIFE AND LIVING

GILBERT GRIERSON

The View From Goak Hill: A Christian's Perspective on Life and Living

Copyright © 2016 by Hayes Press

All rights reserved. Printed in the United Kingdom. No part of this book may be used or reproduced in any manner whatsoever without written permission except in the case of brief quotations embodied in critical articles or reviews.

Unless otherwise indicated, all Scripture references are from the New King James Version® (NKJV®). Copyright © 1982 Thomas Nelson, Inc. Used by permission.

The following Bible versions are also used as indicated throughout:
- 'ESV' - the ESV® Bible (The Holy Bible, English Standard Version®), Copyright © 2001 by Crossway, a publishing ministry of Good News Publishers. Used by permission. All rights reserved.
- 'NIV' - the New International Version®, NIV® Copyright © 1973, 1978, 1984, 2011 by Biblica, Inc.™ Used by permission. All rights reserved;
- 'RV' - the Revised Version, 1885 (Public Domain);
- 'KJV' - the King James Version, 1611 (Public Domain).

Published by Hayes Press (www.hayespress.org), The Barn, Flaxlands, Royal Wootton Bassett, Wiltshire, UK SN4 8DY 01793 850598

ISBN: 9781911433019

First Edition: June 2016

10 9 8 7 6 5 4 3 2 1

DEDICATION

"The View From Goak Hill" is dedicated to my lovely and patient wife, Sue, whom God chose for me to be a "joint heir of the grace of life" (1 Peter 3:7). Shortly after we were married in 1980, we committed to memory the following Bible verses while travelling on a number 36 bus between Leeds and Ripon in Yorkshire, England: "Be ye free from the love of money; content with such things as ye have: for himself hath said, I will in no wise fail thee or forsake thee. So that with good courage we say, 'The Lord is my helper; I will not fear: What shall man do unto me?'" (Heb.13:6 RV) These verses of Scripture continue to be some of those we rest our lives together on, as we travel heavenward, by God's amazing grace.

Bus Number 36

There've been stops along the way, dear,
But we'll get there yet!
The narrow road before us,
That we've travelled since we met.
The lessons we have learned, dear,
And the bridges we have crossed,
Are part of God's great plan, dear,
Secured by Jesus at great cost.
As we travel on in faith, dear,
On Him our eyes we fix,
Remembering we held hands, dear,
On bus number 36!

Gilbert Grierson, May 2016.

PREFACE

In "The View From Goak Hill", Gilbert draws on his experience of working in a variety of occupations, including being an "apprentice" to one of the last traditional country craftsman potters in the north of England. Having had a life-changing experience in Israel in 1975 when, by faith, he accepted that Jesus had fulfilled everything necessary for salvation to be offered as a free gift, he re-trained as a nurse and has worked until retirement in hospitals and hospices in the north of England and in Northern Ireland, where he currently lives with his wife, Sue, not far from Goak Hill in County Tyrone. They have one son, Danny.

Gilbert still "makes a few pots out of clay" as a hobby, but his major goal in life since 1975 has been to share the "good news" that he discovered in a Gideon's Bible which he took to Israel and that has brought him hope and a purpose in life.

"God opened my eyes to see truth that brought me peace and hope. Now I look at the world differently. These writings are my attempt to pass on what I see from my "Goak Hill" to ordinary people like myself who are troubled about the world we live in and are looking for answers."

In some chapters, Gilbert draws lessons from the world around him and tries to see life from a Christian perspective - this is the "outward look", from "Goak Hill." In others, Gilbert takes an "inward look" into Scripture to see what God says about our lives, and how we should be living in the 21st Century.

CONTENTS

THE VIEW FROM GOAK HILL i

DEDICATION iii

PREFACE iv

CONTENTS 5

1: THE VIEW FROM GOAK HILL 9

2: SAFE HOME 11

3: THE OVERGROWN PATH 14

4: O FOOLISH GALATIANS! 17

5: HOW LONG? 20

6: FISHING FOR MEN 23

7: WHAT IS YOUR OCCUPATION? 26

8: GOD'S GRACE – A PERSONAL TESTIMONY 29

9: SETTING THE COMPASS 32

10: WATCHERS AT THE CROSS – THE ORPHAN CRY 35

11: WATCHERS AT THE CROSS – HIS FACE 38

12: WATCHERS AT THE CROSS – HIS LOVE 41

13: OUT OF THE FURNACE 44

14: USEFUL! 46

15: HOLDEN 48

16: THE PEACOCK 51

17: REMEMBER THE SWALLOWS 54

18: UPSIDE-DOWN VALUES – THE POOR IN SPIRIT 57

19: SPIRITUAL SECURITY 60

20: FIRE! FIRE! 63

21: THE FIRST KISS 67

22: TWITCHING 70

23: UNSOUGHT 73

24: A REALITY CHECK 77

25: BETRAYED! 80

26: NO CUTBACKS 83

27: TO THE SCRAPHEAP! 86

28: NOBBUT CLAY! 88

29: UNDER MY NOSE! 91

30: SEAMLESS 94

31: HALLMARKS OF WORSHIP 98

32: MALACHI – THE PROPHET WITH A WAKE-UP CALL 102

33: APPOINTED TIMES 107

34: FRUIT 109

35: FOR TIMES OF BEREAVEMENT 112

36: THE SECRETS OF THE HEART 117

37: DO YOU LOVE ME? (PART ONE) 122

38: DO YOU LOVE ME? (PART TWO) 127

39: DO YOU LOVE ME? (PART THREE) 130

40: LOSING HEART 134

41: THE BREATH OF GOD 136

42: CARES 139

43: GHOSTS 142

44: STEP BACK 146

45: WHAT WILL IT BE? 149

46: FLY AWAY HOME 151

47: A STRING OF BLESSINGS 155

48: DISTANT PEAKS 157

SET FREE IN ISRAEL: GILBERT'S STORY 158

MORE TITLES FROM HAYES PRESS 161

ABOUT HAYES PRESS 164

1: THE VIEW FROM GOAK HILL

The buzzards fly high over Goak Hill*. On a sunny summer's day in Ireland's emerald isle a whole family of these birds of prey can be seen circling, rising and falling on the thermals, calling to each other with their distinctive cry, while scanning the fields and woods beneath for their lunch (although I sometimes think that they just enjoy flying for the fun of it!).

Nothing misses their amazingly comprehensive vision, not the slightest movement of the tiniest shrew in the long grass. There was one summer's day when I spied a lone buzzard a hundred or so feet over Goak Hill. Then looking higher, attracted by the noise, I saw an army helicopter, possibly surveying the area beneath, with their long-range cameras. ("The Troubles", as they are known locally in Northern Ireland, had subsided by this time, but the army were still present in the area, manning road blocks and doing aerial patrols.)

Then, as my eyes scanned higher still, some thousands of feet above both the buzzard and the hovering helicopter, I spied a passenger jet, a sliver of silver reflecting the sun with its give-away vapour trail. I imagined passengers, chatting, sipping coffee, and looking down on the green countryside, the lochs, the rolling hills, whilst speeding westwards on the main east-west, trans-Atlantic passenger jet route, bound for somewhere in Canada or America. On such a day they would have a great view! But not much hope of them spotting a tiny shrew in the long grass on

Goak Hill thousands of feet below!

Let's consider for a moment, at the beginning of these personal observations on life and living, that there is One, indescribably higher than buzzards, helicopters or jumbo-jets, and definitely higher than me, whose look not only takes in the whole universe, but Who is also described in the Bible as noticing even when a sparrow falls to the ground (Matt.10:29). And this is the God who takes notice of you and me! So, no hiding - but, thankfully, no need to hide!

As believers on the Lord Jesus Christ, God's Son, God is on our side. And He wants us to try and see the world from His perspective, as far as we are able; to try to make sense of all the pain and suffering that are found in the world; to see where mankind has come from and where we are headed; how we are to respond to the global and very personal issues of the day; and especially how our God and Saviour, Jesus, want us to live, with all our myopia, as a Christian in His world.

If the following set of writings, written over about sixteen years, (with no thought of being collected together inside one cover) in any way help to focus the view from your particular "Goak Hill", then we'll give the glory to God! After all, our God not only created the hills in the beginning, along with the buzzards, but also the eyes to see them and the lens to focus our vision. He created our minds to understand and to do His will, and faith to accept and believe what we cannot understand.

(*Goak Hill is in County Tyrone, Northern Ireland, over-looking the Blackwater river.)

2: SAFE HOME

It was the annual school cross-country race at the school I attended in Yorkshire. Different teams were competing; the gruelling course involved running alongside a river for a few miles, across a bridge, back along the opposite river bank, up a steep flight of steps to reach the top of a cliff and finally onto the school sports field to the finish line with most of the school cheering on the finishers as they crossed the line. After setting off with collective enthusiasm, the course soon sorted out the 'men' from the 'boys', and I found myself plodding along somewhere towards the back of the bunch of runners. As the pain began to set in, only one thought remained in my mind: 'Get to the line and finish.' The words, 'Nearly there; nearly there,' accompanied the rhythm of my heavy feet and pounding heart. And then the finish line was in sight at last, and a few of the crowd were still there to clap in the last of the stragglers as they came up the home straight and crossed the line. Safe home - and I wasn't the last, as I'd feared!

'Safe home.' Years later, in a nursing home in Northern Ireland, poor Nancy would always say that to me as I left her room, having said goodnight to her at the end of my shift. Nancy, who was living out the rest of her years needing full nursing care, who couldn't even turn herself over in bed, but who was still able to enjoy a laugh - a bit of 'craic', as the Irish call it - to lighten her days spent limited within the confines of a small room and a weakening body. It wasn't until some time later, when I was driving through a small village on the north Antrim coast of Ireland, near the Giant's Causeway, that I came across Nancy's farewell words again. They were on a signpost at the side of the road for motorists to read as they left the village: SAFE HOME. So that's where Nancy got it from. It was a traditional Irish blessing when parting with friends.

As a nurse I have sat with a lot of terminally ill people as they have reached the end of their 'race'. Sometimes there seems to be nothing left to do, but to sit holding their hand, trusting that that touch at least will be the source of some comfort. I know in my mind and in my heart that I am going to heaven when I die because I have trusted in the Lord Jesus as my Saviour. Jesus said, "In my Father's house are many rooms; ...I am going there to prepare a place for you" (1). And Paul expressed a preference "to be away from the body and at home with the Lord" (2). I know the last finishing straight could be a hard one, possibly with pain. But I also know that He will be there to meet me and that all the pain and the sadness will be over.

One year, while attending a Christian teen camp situated quite close to the Giant's Causeway, in one of the meetings the camp leader gave us a small piece of paper and a pencil. He asked us all to imagine being on an aircraft for a journey and the captain comes on the intercom to say that a serious emergency has occurred and the plane is about to crash. 'You have 10 seconds left to live,' Harry the leader informed us. 'You have a small piece of paper and a pencil. What message will you write before the plane crashes, in the hope it will be found in the wreckage afterwards?' I gave it a moment's thought and then wrote on my piece of paper:

SAFE HOME. JOHN 3:16

That Bible verse gives me the certainty that, whatever happens to me, I will be 'safe home' with my Saviour: "For God so loved the world that he gave his one and only Son that whoever believes in him shall not perish but have eternal life (3)."

References (all Scripture references from the NIV): (1) Jn.14:2 (2) 2 Cor.5:8 (3) Jn.3:16

3: THE OVERGROWN PATH

When we first moved into our old farmhouse in Northern Ireland, it had been empty for about three years and the garden resembled a jungle. Pushing the jungle back was a major challenge! One area was covered in weeds, but once cut back it revealed a hidden path running down from the house alongside the trees. We cleared the path and clearly marked one edge of it by setting up an old cartwheel.

Four years have passed since that path was cleared, and because we felt that the garden was too big to keep all of it tended, we drew an invisible line and said, 'All within this line we will upkeep; outside is left to nature.' That path fell back outside the line! I looked at it the other day, or at least where it should be! The nettles and weeds have reclaimed it and the old cartwheel is only just visible above the undergrowth.

I wonder if that's true of the life that you used to live for the Lord? The path of service that you trod was clearly marked, much used, an important part of your life. Then gradually things began to drop off. Serving the Lord didn't seem to be so important, other things crept in and little by little the path of service fell into disuse. Soon it was almost out of sight and out of mind. Almost, but not quite, lost! Has the Lord been pulling at your heart-strings recently, saying: "Stand in the way, and see, and ask for the old paths, where the good way is; and walk in it, then you will find rest for your souls" (1)?

The path is still there, much overgrown, but only waiting to be cleared and put to use again. It doesn't matter much if an old path in our too-big garden is given back to be a highway for mice, slugs and caterpillars. But if thorns and thistles are allowed to choke our clear identity as Christians, if we merge into the undergrowth of a world that has despised and rejected the Lord Jesus, then we have lost something precious, including present rest for our souls. If so, who can estimate the grief caused to the heart of the One who said, "Come to me all you who labour and are heavy laden, and I will give you rest" (2) and then went to the cross to pay the penalty that our sins deserved? He finished His work to obtain rest for us, to be given as a gift as we come in faith, and then to be found as we take up His yoke of service to follow Him.

With unfathomable sadness the Father watches and waits for the lost child who wanders abroad, squandering precious time and gifts on the broken things of this present world that cannot last, and meanwhile the path of service, that, if walked, would bring eternal imperishable blessings, grows increasingly choked and neglected. Is that you? Take heart! The Father in the parable that Jesus told in Luke 15:11-32 never stopped hoping and watching; the undergrowth can still be cut back and the ancient paths of blessing found and walked again.

'Repent' is a biblical word and it is the first and essential step to rediscovering the old paths. It means 'a change of heart' or 'an about turn'. Turning back to the Lord takes an about turn, a conscious decision to put things right. Why not take up the spiritual scythe, strimmer and anything else that you need to clear the years of weeds and find again the ancient path of service.

Christian friends will help you as you seek to rediscover the Bible and in it the One who never gave up on you. All these years He stood at a closed door at the end of an overgrown path, gently knocking and saying, "Behold, I stand at the door and knock. If anyone hears my voice and opens the door, I will come in to him and dine with him, and he with me" (3).

References: (1) Jer.6:16 (2) Matt.11:28 (3) Rev.3:20

4: O FOOLISH GALATIANS!

Our guide had not led us very far before he got us lost. He had a guidebook but he didn't study it very carefully. He had never walked the route himself first, so he was not familiar with the way he was supposed to take us. At the time there were a lot of distractions in York as the city was in the run-up to Christmas, with attractions such as medieval street markets and craft fairs to see. So we lost the route we were supposed to take around the 'snickleways' (the narrow streets, courtyards and alleys) of the historic city of York in northern England, having departed from following the guidebook which gave details of the walk and what to look out for. But it didn't matter anyway. We enjoyed our visit and explored the narrow streets and markets and marvelled as we stood in the majestic Minster, the beautiful jewel at the heart of the city.

But the experience did underline in my mind how important it is for us, as Christians, to stick to the Book, and to follow its instructions very closely and carefully. There is a prescribed path to follow that God has traced out for us as followers of our Lord Jesus Christ. It is the way of truth (1). It is no wonder that the early disciples of the Lord were described in Acts as being of the Way (2). Jesus Himself said, "I am the way, the truth, and the life" (3).

What is the consequence of going 'off road' in Christian experience? It can be very serious. In the case of the believers in Galatia to whom Paul wrote his letter, they had deviated from the way of truth in respect of the very means by which they had received their salvation. This was a very serious matter indeed, striking at the heart of the truth of the gospel that Paul was laying as a foundation in every place he visited and preached.

They had taken their eyes off the truth that justification is by faith alone (4), and that it is complete in its work of declaring the believer to be righteous in the same way that Abraham was declared to be righteous in the sight of God through his faith and not through his works (5). Nothing needs to be added to the crosswork of Christ to obtain salvation (6), certainly not the keeping of the Old Covenant law. It is also true that nothing can be subtracted from His finished and completed work.

How foolish to lose sight of this essential truth that affects the whole of a believer's subsequent life and service! Paul described departure from this truth as turning away "…from Him who called you in the grace of Christ, to a different gospel" (7) - a very serious situation indeed. The Galatians needed the strong, loving words of Paul to get them back on track:

"O foolish Galatians! Who has bewitched you that you should not obey the truth, before whose eyes Jesus Christ was clearly portrayed among you as crucified?" (8).

"Stand fast therefore in the liberty by which Christ has made us free, and do not be entangled again with a yoke of bondage" (9).

"You have become estranged from Christ, you who attempt to be justified by law; you have fallen from grace" (10).

"You ran well. Who hindered you from obeying the truth?" (11).

Strong words from Paul, but he was in fighting spirit to make sure the foundation stayed in place in the work that God had given him to do as an apostle of Jesus Christ. An urgent restoration job was needed in Galatia.

Before leaving York on that December day mentioned at the beginning, we stood inside the Minster, that mighty medieval edifice built over 600 years ago. Some time ago, during restoration work, it was discovered that the building had insufficient foundations and was in danger of collapse. An urgent and expensive engineering project was completed and the foundations were reinforced to preserve the building for succeeding generations.

How vital and urgent it is to examine the foundations in our lives and make sure that we are building on the truth found in the Scriptures, and go on following carefully to make sure we reach the finish without being diverted or distracted from the way of the truth found in the Book. Then we will not miss that which is for our eternal blessing in heaven where we will meet the jewel of our quest - the King in all His beauty, who will far surpass anything that is found on earth.

References: (1) 2 Pet.2:2 (2) Acts 9:2; 24:14,22 (3) Jn.14:6 (4) Gal.2:16 (5) Gal.3:6 (6) Gal.2:21 (7) Gal.1:6 (8) Gal.3:1 (9) Gal.5:1 (10) Gal.5:4 (11) Gal.5:7

5: HOW LONG?

The question, "How long?" is often asked in frustration. We don't normally like being asked to wait. Sometimes we are concerned because we know that a long wait can have serious consequences, like waiting for a vital surgical operation to take place. At other times it can just be highly frustrating, like waiting in a traffic jam when we have an important appointment. Usually, when we are forced to wait, it is because we have no choice, and no matter how much we fume and complain, it doesn't make any difference. We live in a generation that increasingly doesn't like to wait. Advertisements promote the idea that we can have what we want now, and pay for it later. Waiting takes patience, and that commodity seems to be in increasingly short supply in our modern society.

To be a farmer, patience is essential. You cannot hurry growing things. To produce crops in harmony with nature takes time. The Bible speaks about the farmer waiting for the harvest, being patient until it has received the necessary seasonal rainfall (1). The Book of Ecclesiastes speaks about there being a season and a time for every purpose under heaven, and about a time to plant and a time to pluck up that which is planted (2). There is no hurrying up of the seasons, and the wise farmer knows that you just have to wait patiently for harvest time to come.

It is only through the discipline of waiting, sometimes having to go through trials at the same time, that the virtue of patience will be developed in us. How patient our Lord Jesus was, as He waited God's time during all those long years in Nazareth. And how patiently He endured the cross, and despised the shame; His divine attributes of patience and meekness gloriously shining out in that Perfect Man, as He underwent suffering at the hands of lawless men. God wants to work those same attributes of patience and meekness into the fabric of our lives, too, as we seek to follow Jesus as Lord and grow more like Him.

In our personal experience we might be brought into situations where we are forced to cry out to God, 'How long?' We are not alone in making this cry. David, in the extremity of his circumstances, cried: "How long, O LORD? Will You forget me forever? How long will You hide Your face from me? How long shall I take counsel in my soul, Having sorrow in my heart daily? How long will my enemy be exalted over me?" (3).

Trials were pressing down on David, just as if he was being crushed in an olive or wine press. He was walking through the valley of the shadow of darkness, where there seemed to be no light, no relief. Do you ever feel like that? His cry to God did not imply any lack of faith on his part. Indeed, he finished his psalm on a note of trust, courage and joy, for he was enabled to look ahead to the end of the matter, just as his Lord would do in a later day and in a vastly darker situation. David was learning the cost of his obedience to his God through the things he was suffering, and at the same time God was working in his life. We are reminded of James's words: "My brethren, count it all joy when you fall into various trials, knowing that the testing of your faith produces patience. But let patience have its perfect work, that you may be perfect and complete, lacking nothing" (4).

We may find ourselves in situations where we, too, cry out,

"How long?" It is not wrong to do so. The Lord understands. In fact, He is the only One who does fully understand. But this experience can be used to produce in us that necessary patience which comes from waiting on God for deliverance. We all, as believers, live in a world that is suffering (5), groaning and travailing while it awaits its deliverance.

In that day of deliverance we, too, will be delivered from the bondage of corruption and receive the redemption of our bodies. This is a tremendous hope; something to look forward to with joyful anticipation. But we need patience. The apostle Paul writes, "For we were saved in this hope, but hope that is seen is not hope; for why does one still hope for what he sees? But if we hope for what we do not see, we eagerly wait for it with perseverance (patience, ESV)" (6).

James also gives us reassurance when he writes, "You also be patient. Establish your hearts, for the coming of the Lord is at hand" (7). There is a coming day when all things will be put right and faith in God will be vindicated. Faith and hope will give way to sight, and sorrow will be turned into joy. Then every 'How long?' shall be answered.

References: (1) Jas.5:7 (2) Eccl.3:1-2 (3) Ps.13:1-2 (4) Jas.1:2-4 (5) Rom.8:22 (6) Rom.8:24-25 (7) Jas.5:8

6: FISHING FOR MEN

There were two fishermen on the jetty at Brantry Lough in County Tyrone, Northern Ireland, on the day I pulled up in the car park and sat watching for a while. The day was wet and two men, one in a wheelchair, sat fishing in the rain. One was fly fishing, his line constantly snaking out over the water, no doubt armed with a skilfully disguised hook. The other man was using a hook with bait attached and sat with eyes riveted to the float for signs of a 'bite'. A good while passed and the fishermen called it a day. I noticed that their keepnets as they lifted them out of the water were empty.

My mind went to the words of the Lord, "Follow Me, and I will make you become fishers of men" (1). We long to see others enjoying God's salvation, serving Him in His kingdom, and watching and waiting for the Lord Jesus to return. Desiring to fulfil the great commission given in Matthew 28:19-20, we make great efforts to fish for men and women, planning and thinking up new ways to bring the fish into the net (or on to the hook!).

In trying to make our efforts productive, we work together to reach out prayerfully and sincerely to those around us. Yet, so often at the end of the day the nets are empty! What could be wrong? In fishing for men and women technique will never be enough on its own. Whether preaching in a traditional gospel service, running an informal introductory Bible teaching video course or personally witnessing one-to-one, it's only when the

Lord is at work that the nets will fill.

Conviction of sin, the new birth, assurance of salvation and revelation of truth are all the work of God through the Word of God, accompanied by the gracious and powerful operation of the Holy Spirit. In relation to fruit-bearing, Jesus said, "Without Me you can do nothing" (2). In regard to fishing for men and women we must depend on God. If God is not at work all our efforts will be in vain. Therefore, before any successful fishing begins, there must be earnest intercession to God for a mighty working of His Spirit in the hearts of those we seek to reach.

I am reminded of a biography I read about J.O. Fraser, a China Inland Mission worker stationed in Yunnan Province, China, in the early 1900's (3). His earnest efforts to reach the tribespeople of that land bore no fruit for many years. Then after years of prayer at home and abroad, and faithful preaching of the gospel around the villages, suddenly there was 'mountain rain'. God was at work! Fraser experienced the joy of realizing that God's time had come. Earnest prayer was at last being answered. Tribespeople began turning to Christ in village after village where previously there had been only resistance or indifference. Souls were being saved and Fraser himself was able to stand back, as increasing numbers of 'fish' were being swept into the net by the sovereign power of God, until the nets were breaking. Fraser's many years of faithful preaching of the Word of God around the mountain villages had finally been rewarded. He stood aside and saw 'the salvation of the LORD', as in the days of Moses (4).

That brings us back to that other quality all fishermen - those by Brantry Lough and those fishing for men and women - need: patience! If the nets are to fill today, then it will be a combination of the right fishermen or women, in the right spiritual condition, in the right place with the right message, waiting patiently for the right moment for God to begin His sovereign work.

Remember the 153 fish that Peter pulled to shore that unforgettable day by the Sea of Galilee (5)? Now that was something which was the Lord's doing, and it was marvellous in the eyes of those disciples who had laboured all night and caught nothing! What made the difference? The Lord was there, guiding the disciples out to the right place to fish and drawing fish into the net, just as He, and He alone, is able to draw men and women to Himself for salvation, then and now. He has not changed and in some areas of this world earnest, diligent fishers of men supported by praying co-workers are still experiencing the joy of pulling in full nets, giving glory to the One who said, "Lo, I am with you always, even to the end of the age" (6).

References: (1) Mk.1:17 (2) Jn.15:5 (3) Crossman, E., Mountain Rain, A biography of James O. Fraser, O.M.F. Books 1982 (4) Ex.14:13 (5) Jn.21:11 (6) Matt.28:20

7: WHAT IS YOUR OCCUPATION?

Most of us have forms to fill in at some point in our lives. Included among the questions almost certainly will be the one above. There would be a variety of answers: professional, managerial, manual - from sales manager to doctor, nurse to housewife and mother. There are many honourable occupations for Christians to follow.

The question was asked of Jonah on board a ship heading for Tarshish, "What is your occupation?" (1). Jonah should have been heading for Nineveh with a message from the Lord of crucial importance to the people of that great city. It was the second of five questions as the sailors urgently cross-examined Jonah in their attempt to discover the reason for the furious storm that was threatening the ship and their lives. He told them, "I am a Hebrew, and I fear the LORD, the God of heaven, who made the sea and the dry land" (2). The terrified sailors "knew that he fled from the presence of the LORD, because he had told them" (3).

In the New Testament we read of another ship and another prophet: this time the apostle Paul is bound for Rome, a prisoner of Christ Jesus for the sake of the gospel (4). During the sea voyage another storm was encountered and the ship full of sailors, Roman soldiers and prisoners, were all fearful for their lives. All except Paul that is. Paul, as an ambassador for Jesus Christ, was taking God's message of salvation to the very heart of the mighty Roman empire in absolute obedience to his Master's commandment. He had nothing on his conscience to make him fearful or ashamed. In his letter written earlier to the Christians at Rome he described himself as "a bondservant of Jesus Christ, called to be an apostle, separated (set apart) to the gospel of God" (5).

There was no doubt in Paul's mind as to his occupation! His was the most honourable occupation; not just a servant of a king but of the King of kings. In the same letter and chapter he also spells out his absolute confidence in the message he was carrying and for which he was prepared to offer his life: "For I am not ashamed of the gospel of Christ, for it is the power of God to salvation for everyone who believes, for the Jew first and also for the Greek" (6).

In Luke 19:13, in the parable that the Lord Jesus told to His disciples as His death on the Cross drew near, the nobleman said to the ten servants he was leaving, "Occupy till I come" (KJV). Should not those words be bound upon the forehead and written upon the heart of every disciple as a daily reminder of what we should be about? We may not have been called to travel to distant countries as pioneer missionaries, but should it not be the prime concern of every disciple of the Lord to be about the King's business in whatever work department He may have placed us? There let us be His faithful witnesses in deed and word as servants called to a mighty task, a most honourable occupation, a responsibility not to be run away from.

In one of her poems, 'In Any Office', Amy Carmichael refers to the potters who "dwell at Netaim and Gederah; there they dwelt with the king for his work" (7). How would they have answered the question, 'What is your occupation'? Would they have said, 'We are potters' or, 'We are servants of the king'? 'What is your occupation?' is a good question to ask ourselves as we go out to work in the morning. Amy in her inimitable way writes:

> My potter's wheel is where
> I see a desk and office chair,
> And well I know the Lord is there.
> And all my work is for a King... (8)

Whatever job we may do, let us look beyond our immediate employer and do our work "as bondservants of Christ…as to the Lord" (9) and strive to be fully occupied as His witnesses until the Lord comes, heeding the Lord's words in the parable, "occupy till I come".

References: (1) Jonah 1:8 (2) Jonah 1:9 (3) Jonah 1:10 (4) Acts 27 (5) Rom.1:1 (6) Rom.1:16 (7) 1 Chron.4:23 (8) Amy Carmichael, SPCK, Towards Jerusalem (9) Eph.6:6-7

8: GOD'S GRACE – A PERSONAL TESTIMONY

In 1980, my wife and I were presented with a picture by the 'Young People's Meeting' of the churches of God in the north-west of England, following a long-established tradition, to mark the occasion of our marriage. That picture is of the sea and waves breaking on a sandy shore, with mountains in the background. A Bible text above it all reads: "MY GRACE IS SUFFICIENT FOR THEE" (2 Cor.12:9 KJV).

That picture has hung in our bedroom, wherever we have lived, ever since - a well-appreciated gift. There's many a morning when I wake and look up at that picture and its text. I never know what a day is going to bring or what demands are going to be put upon me, but those words have been a constant help to me. They were spoken by the Lord to the apostle Paul personally, but they have been a great source of encouragement to me and, I'm sure, to many others also over the years.

In my work as a nurse, and for some years nursing terminally-ill patients, I have found myself in many situations where I have needed help and strength to fulfil my role, to work with others in giving care to those going through the experience of serious illness and facing up to death, and with giving support to grieving families and friends. At times it has not been easy. Nurses and others in the caring professions (and I'm certain in other jobs, too) often find themselves drained psychologically and emotionally, as well as physically. There is a constant danger of burnout. There is an ongoing need to be sympathetic. Working in a secular nursing system there is also the constant danger of accepting the values and work ethic of non-Christian colleagues who, though excellent nurses in other respects, may regard spiritual care as very low in their order of priorities. Then there is always the need for courage when appropriate moments do come for personal witness.

What helps in such situations? The same as helped Paul in coping with his afflictions and his trials - God's grace. I have found over the years that the Lord's promise is true. His grace has been sufficient, and through it the difficulties have been overcome. At times of personal failure, forgiveness has also been available, and restoration of the joy of the Lord, all through God's grace.

I have not personally faced up to very serious illness in my own life, but increasing years do bring their own particular needs, and I am very thankful to swing my legs out of bed in the morning, look up at the picture, read the text and ask God to strengthen me for yet another day. If and when times of weakness and illness do come, in God's will, and increasing dependence on the care of others, I know one thing will not have changed: God's grace. It will always be sufficient.

It may be, as you read this, that you may be wondering how you are going to cope with a particular circumstance that has come into your own life, be it illness or some other trial. I would like my testimony to direct you to the Word of God, particularly concerning His grace. Whatever happens, it will be sufficient for you, because He has promised. I have given out this little poem to many patients over the years and to their families. May it be a help to you, too.

What God Hath Promised

God hath not promised skies always blue,
Flower-strewn pathways all our lives through;
God hath not promised sun without rain,
Joy without sorrow, peace without pain.
But God hath promised strength for the day,
Rest for the labour, light for the way,
Grace for the trials, help from above,
Unfailing sympathy, undying love.
(Annie Johnson Flint, 1919)

9: SETTING THE COMPASS

We were visiting a small fishing harbour on the west coast of Ireland. Moored at the quayside was a yacht waiting to go out to sea. The size of the wheel that steered the yacht was impressive, but what caught my eye was the instrument that took prominence next to the wheel: a ship's compass, an essential piece of equipment for navigating the seas, with its needle always indicating a fixed point and the captain able to set his course by it, aided by his navigation charts.

That reminds me of our Christian lives. We need fixed points to steer by. Moses had one. We read of it in Hebrews: "By faith Moses, …choosing rather to suffer affliction with the people of God than to enjoy the passing pleasures of sin, esteeming the reproach of Christ greater riches than the treasures in Egypt; for he looked to the reward. By faith he forsook Egypt, not fearing the wrath of the king; for he endured as seeing Him who is invisible" (1). Moses' eye was on the invisible and by it he set his compass, and that determined the direction and goal of his life, regardless of the consequences.

Jim Elliot was another man of God who had set his compass and lived his life accordingly. He wrote the words, 'He is no fool who gives what he cannot keep to gain what he cannot lose.' In his efforts to win the Auca Indians of South America for the

Lord, he eventually gave his all, paying the ultimate price of his life, killed by those primitive people he was seeking to reach, along with his fellow missionaries (2). He was no loser. He only gave what he could not keep. His gain was eternal. We all have things to give and a very wise and generous Christian neighbour of ours says quite frequently, "There are no pockets in a shroud," meaning, of course, that we cannot take our material possessions with us when we die.

The set of the unseen compass is so clearly defined in the words of Scripture, "...we do not look at the things which are seen, but at the things which are not seen. For the things that are seen are temporary, but the things which are not seen are eternal" (3).

Amy Carmichael of Dohnavur in South India had her compass set on the unseen when she was still a young woman living in Ireland. She describes in her biography 'Gold Cord' (4) an incident that happened one wet day in Belfast. She and her family met a pathetic old woman carrying a bundle. Amy and her brothers felt led to help her with her bundle and for Amy, a young girl, in the sight of a lot of respectable well-dressed church-goers, it was a very embarrassing experience. Just as they were passing a drinking fountain at the side of the road, a scripture flashed into Amy's mind: "Gold, silver, precious stones, wood, hay, stubble; every man's work shall be made manifest: for the day shall declare it, because it shall be revealed by fire; and the fire shall try every man's work of what sort it is. If any man's work abide..." 'We went on. I said nothing to anyone, but I knew that something had happened that had changed life's values. Nothing could ever matter again but the things that were eternal' (4).

Later that day Amy shut herself in her room, talked to God

and settled once and for all the pattern of her future life. Her compass had been set. What about us? Are the things that are eternal the things that matter most to us? Sometimes God has to work in our lives to change our values. God wants us to gain what we cannot lose by giving what we cannot keep, and to set our compasses on the invisible and the eternal.

We, as disciples of our Lord Jesus Christ, want to be as He was in the days of His pilgrimage. His compass was resolutely fixed, first to set Him on course for the cross; "therefore I have set my face like a flint, and I know that I shall not be ashamed" (5) and beyond that, He saw "the joy that was set before Him" (6) when, having put shame and spitting behind Him, He would sit down at the right hand of the throne of God. And as pilgrims, compass in hand, we too should be always "looking unto Jesus, the author and finisher of our faith" (6) and, come what may, keep our eyes fixed on Him.

References: (1) Heb.11:24-27 (2) 'Through Gates of Splendour' by Elisabeth Elliot. Hodder & Stoughton 1957 (3) 2 Cor.4:18 (4) 'Gold Cord, the Story of a Fellowship', Chapter 1. Published by S.P.C.K., 1932 (5) Is.50:7 (6) Heb.12:2

10: WATCHERS AT THE CROSS – THE ORPHAN CRY

I invite you to draw near with me to watch reverently at the cross of our Lord Jesus and to see the love of God unfold.

It is about the ninth hour and Jesus cries out with a loud voice, 'My God, my God, why hast thou forsaken me' (1), and, shortly afterwards, He lays down His own life, saying, 'Father, into thy hands I commend my spirit' (2).

Earlier that day the soldiers of the governor (Pilate) had subjected the Lord to a mock coronation, nailed Him to the cross, and set up over His head His accusation, THIS IS JESUS THE KING OF THE JEWS. Two robbers were crucified with Him, one on the right hand and one on the left. Passersby hurled their insults at Him, goading Him to come down from the cross and save Himself, if He really was the Son of God! The Chief Priests with the teachers and elders also mocked Him. "He saved others," they say, "himself he cannot save" (3).

Initially, the robbers who were being crucified with Him also heaped insults on Him, until one of them, accepting his own guilt and the justness of the punishment he was receiving, but convinced that Jesus had done nothing wrong, said to Jesus, "Jesus, remember me when thou comest in thy kingdom."

"Today shalt thou be with me in Paradise," Jesus replies (4). Between the sixth and ninth hours there is darkness over all the land, for the sun stops shining. During the hours of darkness, one robber is hanging on his cross, still in his sins, while the other robber also hangs there, his life slowly ebbing away, but resting on the promise of Jesus.

Unseen by the watchers at the cross, during those hours of darkness a transference takes place. The sins of the robber who has turned to the Lord in repentance and faith are placed on the Lord Jesus. We remember the scapegoat on whose head the High Priest placed his hands and confessed the sins of the people of Israel annually on the Day of Atonement. Then the living goat was taken away into the wilderness to a solitary place and released bearing the sins of the people. "And the goat shall bear upon him all their iniquities unto a solitary land ('place' - NIV) and he shall let the goat go in the wilderness" (5). That unprotected goat was left in the wilderness, probably to be found and set upon by wild beasts. What plaintive cries might have been uttered before it met its violent end, forsaken in a solitary place? As Jesus cries out on the cross, do we hear the voice of One crying out in a solitary place, "My God, my God, why hast thou forsaken me?"

> How deep the Father's love for us,
> How vast beyond all measure,
> That He should give His only Son,
> To make a wretch His treasure.
> How great the pain of searing loss,
> The Father turns His face away,
> As wounds which mar the Chosen One,
> Bring many sons to glory. (Stuart Townend)

What cost to the Father, who "spared not his own Son, but delivered him up for us all" (6). What cost to the Son, "who was wounded for our transgressions" (7). As the scapegoat on the Day of Atonement was bearing the sins of the people, so the Lord Jesus wasn't just carrying the sins of the one robber, but "the LORD hath laid on him the iniquity of us all" (8).

> Our sins were laid upon Him,
> And thus our debt was paid (9).

On the cross, He was being forsaken that we might never be forsaken; cut off that we might be brought in; laying down even His life to cancel our debt and give us everlasting life; having nothing so that we might have everything and one day, be brought by Him, as sons, to glory.

> O God, our hearts united
> Would praise Thee for Thy Son (9).

References (all Scripture references from the RV): (1) Matt.27:46 (2) Lk.23:46 (3) Matt.27:42 (4) Lk.23:42-43 (5) Lev.16:22 (6) Rom.8:32 (7) Is.53:5 (8) Is.53:6 (9) Hymn 101, Psalms Hymns and Spiritual Songs, J.B. Belton

11: WATCHERS AT THE CROSS – HIS FACE

O sacred Head once wounded,
With grief and pain weighed down,
How scornfully surrounded
With thorns, Thine only crown! (1)

We continue to watch and meditate at the cross. When the soldiers of the governor crucified Jesus, Matthew tells us that "they kept watch over Him there" (2). We join them there. What do we see? Certainly the soldiers see a man bearing all the marks of the violence that they and others had inflicted upon Him. They see no outward beauty in Him - just the opposite.

At the house of the High Priest the previous night, after questioning, the officers or guards had spat in Jesus' face. Then they had blindfolded Him and struck Him about the face with their fists, saying, "Prophesy! Who is the one who struck you?" (3). The soldiers see spittle and bruising about the face of the Lord Jesus. After Jesus had been questioned by Pilate, the soldiers of the governor had stripped and robed Him as a King, mocking Him with a crown made of sharp piercing thorns placed on His head. Then they had taken the reed or staff that they had put into His right hand and smitten Him on the head with it.

Then they had led Him away to crucify Him and having shared out His garments they sat and watched Him there, suffering in grief and pain.

> How art Thou pale with anguish,
> With sore abuse and scorn!
> How does that visage languish,
> Which once was bright as morn! (4)

Writing prophetically, Isaiah had said, "Just as many were astonished at you, so His visage was marred more than any man, and His form more than the sons of men" (5). Also speaking through Isaiah, the Lord Himself had anticipated His own suffering, saying, "I gave My back to those who struck Me, and my cheeks to those who plucked out the beard; I did not hide my face from shame and spitting" (6). In their unrestrained violence those who tortured the Lord Jesus had even wrenched out parts of the beard from His face. Such cruelty! Such love to allow it!

So no beauty is seen by the watchers, but a face ripped; a head bruised and torn. They do not see the sorrow and love that, woven together, 'composed so rich a crown'. They do not know what it was costing the Holy One of God to bear the sin of the world and to weave a rich garment of righteousness to cover our nakedness and guilt. But what do we see, as watchers at the cross? Just a suffering man, or the glory of God? Paul, in his letter to the Corinthian church, wrote, "For it is the God who commanded light to shine out of darkness, who has shone in our hearts to give the light of the knowledge of the glory of God in the face of Jesus Christ" (7).

Glory in the face of Jesus Christ! Even in the face of God's

Son on the cross? Yes, especially there in the terrible darkness of Calvary and against the dark background of man's inhumanity, shone out the glory of suffering Love, as the heart of God was revealed, for God is love. At a later date, the Apostle John in his vision of the Lord in the book of The Revelation, saw Jesus, and "His countenance was like the sun shining in its strength" (8). On the cross that light was blotted out for a short while so that our sins might be blotted out eternally. What cause for thankfulness and praise! So, let us who have had light revealed to us, each say as we watch at the cross:

> What language shall I borrow,
> To praise Thee, heavenly Friend,
> For this Thy dying sorrow,
> Thy pity without end? (9)

References: (1), (4) & (9) Translated by Dr. J.W. Alexander from P. Gerhardt & Bernard of Clairvaux (2) Matt.27:36 (3) Lk.22:64 (5) Is.52:14 (6) Is.50:6 (7) 2 Cor.4:6 (8) Rev.1:16

12: WATCHERS AT THE CROSS – HIS LOVE

"I will enter His gates with thanksgiving in my heart, I will enter His courts with praise (1)."

Again we join the watchers at the cross. Jesus has just cried out with a loud voice, and knowing that all things have now been finished, He says, "I thirst!" (2). One of those who stand nearby dips a sponge into a vessel of wine vinegar and raises it on a rod of hyssop and puts it to Jesus' mouth. Having tasted it, Jesus says, "It is finished!" (3). In their final act of mockery they give Him vinegar to drink - sour wine! In His first miracle at Cana of Galilee, Jesus had changed water into the best wine at the wedding feast, which was in keeping with the character of all His words and works: the very best. His final act upon the cross is to take the very worst that men could give Him - vinegar, sour wine!

This, too, was in fulfilment of Scripture: "They also gave me gall for my food, and for my thirst they gave me vinegar to drink" (4). This same passage begins with the words, "Reproach has broken my heart, and I am full of heaviness; I looked for someone to take pity, but there was none; and for comforters, but I found none" (4). Vinegar! The final reproach heaped upon the Son of God, and nothing and no-one to comfort Him in His hour of distress. How can sinful creatures like ourselves ever hope to plumb the depth of such love? We cannot.

> Such love springs from eternity;
> Such love, streaming through history;
> Such love, fountain of life to me;
> O Jesus, such love. (5)

Yes, we, the watchers at the cross, "love Him because He first loved us" (6). And when did He first love us? We each had a point in time when our love began and grew. Was there a point of time when the Son of God began loving us? "God is love" (7), the apostle John tells us. "I have loved you with an everlasting love" (8), God told Israel through Jeremiah, and we who are members in the Church the Body share equally in that eternal stream of love from which nothing can separate us.

So God has loved us from eternity past. But at the cross the full expression of that love was made known; a love which is endless. "God demonstrates His own love toward us, in that while we were still sinners, Christ died for us" (9). And as we watch the final moments of the Lord Jesus on the cross, we cry out, "Why did He do it?" The answer comes, "that He might bring us to God" (10) as worshippers (11). So let us enter His gates with thanksgiving in our hearts, and enter His courts with praise, for:

> This is the day the Lord hath made,
> He calls the hours His own.
> Let heaven rejoice, let earth be glad,
> And praise surround Thy throne. (12)

References: (1) Lyrics by Leona von Brethorst (2) Jn.19:28 (3) Jn.19:30 (4) Ps.69:20-21 (5) Lyrics by Graham Kendrick (6) 1 Jn.4:19 (7) 1 Jn.4:8 (8) Jer.31:3 (9) Rom.5:8 (10) 1 Pet.3:18 (11) Jn.4:23 (12) Isaac Watts

13: OUT OF THE FURNACE

In parts of Nigeria they still build a traditional bottle-shaped furnace, or kiln, fuelled by wood to fire and finish large earthenware pots to be used for cooking and other essential activities of daily life. I remember many years ago heading into Stoke-on-Trent, centre of the 'Potteries' industrial area in the English midlands. The road wound down through a suburb and all around were the bottle kilns in use at that time, belching out flames and smoke. It was dusk and it seemed like a setting for Dante's Inferno!

There was a furnace built long ago in what is now Iraq. King Nebuchadnezzar hadn't ordered it to be fuelled for pots or bricks, but for three men: Shadrach, Meshach and Abednego (1). They had disobeyed the king's decree to bow down to a false god and in his anger he ordered them to be thrown into a blazing superheated fiery furnace. The men who threw them in themselves perished with the heat, but the three obedient servants of God came out unscathed, with not a hair on their bodies singed! Their God was indeed the great Deliverer, to whom one day every knee must bow, even the knee of the king of Babylon. The furnace only served to glorify God.

As disciples of the Lord Jesus, sometimes there can be a fiery furnace in our experience too. Peter, writing to believers in a largely hostile world, could say, "Beloved, do not think it strange concerning the fiery trial which is to try you" (2). If you are going through a 'fiery trial', a furnace experience, don't be afraid. Paul wrote, "Your life is hidden with Christ in God" (3) and nothing can touch it. The fiery trial is testing "the genuineness of your faith" (4). It is making you into a vessel fit for the Master's use (5).

References: (1) Dan.3 (2) 1 Pet.4:12 (3) Col.3:3 (4) 1 Pet.1:7 (5) 2 Tim.2:21

14: USEFUL!

Sometimes, when I am working on the potter's wheel, the pot on which I'm busy develops a fault and I know it's not going to turn out in the way I intended. In a moment of haste, I am ready to consign it to the waste heap. But sometimes, after reflection, I have continued working with it and after some changes, have been able to rescue it after all. I have a pot on the finished shelf right now that was near to being rejected, but is now ready for some use.

'Profitable' was such a man! He had seemed worthless when he ran away from his master and ended up in Rome. But God the Master Potter had His eye on Onesimus (for that's who he was - see Paul's letter to Philemon), and 'profitable' or 'useful' is the meaning of his name. Paul, in his letter to his dear friend, writes concerning Onesimus the run-away slave, "Formerly he was useless to you, but now he has become useful both to you and to me" (1), a word-play on the slave's name. Saved through the witness of the apostle Paul in prison in Rome, set aside (sanctified) through faith in the Lord Jesus, Onesimus had a new lease of life, and a new purpose to fulfil in the great plan of things.

Let us learn the lesson. Some whom we would be ready to give up on, who would seem to have no useful future in the things of God, whom we would be ready to cast aside as useless, thinking that they are not in the category God would look for, may only need a bit of time and attention to make them useful disciples serving God in His house. With loving care and prayer and diligent teaching, the hand of God can do wonders and one who seemed destined to the rubbish heap can go on to serve to the glory of God, fulfilling some useful task as did Onesimus, the one who became 'USEFUL'!

References: (1) Phm. v.11

15: HOLDEN

At the time of writing, it is a beautiful summer's day. My early morning walk took me by a field of wheat, ripening in the warm sunshine, with the yellow heads bending under the weight of the grain. The field was very quiet, deserted in fact. But I knew that that field would shortly, perhaps in just a few days, be full of activity; workers with a combine harvester, tractors and trailers bringing in the harvest, knowing that the days of opportunity for harvesting will be short.

My mind went back to another field and another time in another land. There, on the outskirts of Bethlehem, the harvest had started. No noisy machinery, but no doubt men wielding sickles or scythes and others gathering the stalks up into bundles to make sheaves. It was the barley harvest time, and amidst the sheaves was a stranger, bending patiently to pick up ears of corn that had fallen here and there. She was Ruth, the Moabitess, gleaning there with the permission and blessing of the lord of that harvest, Boaz, in whose sight she had found grace (1).

Another hot summer's day, a thirsty day for harvesting, and a Man reaping in the fields. This time it's the Lord of the harvest, come down from heaven, who is the reaper. That day in Samaria, by Sychar's well (2), He is harvesting, gleaning a head of fallen corn, a sinful Samaritan woman, graciously drawing her into His storehouse, and gathering many more (3) of the lost souls of Samaria into bundles. In Samaria that day, the fields are "already white for harvest" (4), and the harvest has begun. No need to wait four months!

Holden is an old English word meaning 'held fast'. In Luke 24:16 (KJV and RV) the eyes of the disciples walking to Emmaus were 'holden' as they walked with the Stranger who joined them on the road. Because their eyes were 'restrained', as the NKJV puts it, they did not recognize the Lord Jesus. Later, in the taking, breaking and blessing of the bread at the meal table, Jesus was revealed to them: "their eyes were opened and they knew Him" (v.31).

What is our vision power as this day of God's grace continues? Is it possible that, in respect of the fields which the Lord Jesus described as 'white' or ready for harvesting, our eyes could be 'holden'? Is it possible that we could be blind and careless in regard to the souls that are perishing at our side, "having no hope and without God in the world" (5)?

Is it possible that we have no desire to see them reached with the gospel message that saves? The days of opportunity for harvesting may be short, and the fields, heavy with corn, go unreaped. Do we need to be praying for our eyes to be opened? This is the day of opportunity; no need to wait four more months! Praise God for every disciple who sees enough of the need to be praying earnestly to the Lord of the Harvest to send out labourers into His harvest fields, and praise God for those who have found grace in His eyes to be employed in His work in some way, great or small.

He needs some to be bringing in the bundles and others to be engaged in the personal work of quietly gleaning. But all are working together so that one day, sowers and reapers, including gleaners, will rejoice together, in that day when He "shall doubtless come again with rejoicing, bringing his sheaves with him" (6).

References: (1) Ruth 2:15 (2) Jn.4 (3) Jn.4:41 (4) Jn.4:35 (5) Eph.2:12 (6) Ps. 126:6

16: THE PEACOCK

I stepped out of the front door into the garden for a few minutes of stress-busting fresh air, just to relieve the tension that creeps up on you almost imperceptibly when working on something that is particularly demanding mentally. It makes you realise that breaks in the working day are not just there for the fun of it, but serve a very necessary function.

If you are privileged, as I am, to be able to step out into the fresh country air, breathe deeply, and let the quiet restfulness of a garden, park, or even a tub of flowers calm the spirit, and there be reminded that from everlasting to everlasting God is God and that resting in Him is an essential to peace of mind, then that is a blessed break indeed.

I spent a moment or two looking at the honeysuckle – such beauty and fragrance and yet all it is doing is growing where it has been planted. I wonder if there will be such wonderful perfume in Heaven? I then crossed the lawn to the buddleia bush, with its heads of purple-blue blooms. That's when I saw it! A butterfly resting motionless on a flower head. What colours, what beauty – it must be a Peacock! For a few moments I stood motionless drinking in its beauty and harmony of design while it remained still, feeding on the flower. I noted the lovely balance of the 'peacock' colours, shades of red and yellow, blue and purple, and darker marks on both wings. Just time to observe the sensitive antennae, and then, it was gone, leaving only a memory of its brief appearance.

It reminded me of another lovely appearing: a perfect Man from heaven, eternal and invisible, yet briefly seen amongst the things that are temporal, by the grace of God; something eternal manifested in the flesh and capable of being looked at and wondered at. He settled for a selected moment in the spans of time, just long enough to give the ardent seeker a glimpse of the invisible God; the Creator of all beauty; the great Designer of the Peacock butterfly whose artist's palette is infinite in the variety of its resources, far beyond the range of human perception.

What balance there is in that Man: meekness and majesty; absolute holiness with approachable lowliness; kingly authority, but suffering servant-hood; hatred of sin, yet love of the sinner; the Lion and the Lamb:

> Meekness and majesty,
> Manhood and deity
> In perfect harmony,
> The Man who is God.
> Lord of eternity
> Dwells in humanity;
> Kneels in humility
> And washes our feet.
> (Graham Kendrick)

He came and went, a sensitive Saviour bearing sin on the cross for our sakes. What will it be when He comes to reign! How like the Peacock butterfly and yet how unlike it. 'The Peacock, once summer is over, hibernates until spring comes again, and it re-appears, by which time it is often torn and faded,' my book on butterflies tells me.

Not so with our Lord Jesus; He was glorified with the glory He had with the Father before the foundation of the world. Despite the cross, His beauty is eternally undiminished and is perfectly in place in the beautiful mansions above. The dark marks of the cross only increased His beauty for it added what had not been there before, the marks of Calvary. These reveal the visible hue of the height and depth of the love of God, seen in the fullness of suffering, and the drinking of the cup of suffering that could not have been fuller, for the One in whom dwelt all the fullness of the Godhead bodily. When He is manifested a second time, at His coming to reign, His beauty will be unsurpassed, with no fading, eternally glorious.

17: REMEMBER THE SWALLOWS

I wondered where they all were when it was November in Northern Ireland and the winter was coming on. Only a couple of months previously, I had written about them in my journal, "The swallows are still here at the moment, swooping excitedly about the farmhouse, or perched in a line along the ridge of a nearby barn, twittering together while seeming to warm their backs in the heat of the morning sun rising over Goak Hill to the east."

It was early September then; the sycamore trees were casting a few leaves and there was a hint of autumn in the dew on the grass and the spiders' webs in the hedges. For a few summer months they had entertained us and been part of our lives. They had built their clay nests – one under the eaves just outside our bedroom window. They had dive-bombed Jack the cat as he crossed the yard; he had tried vainly to ignore their sudden sorties, appearing and disappearing like an R.A.F. squadron or a Red Arrows display team at an air show. They amazed us with their ability to fly in and out of broken windows to colonise the empty barns, and they amused us in the middle of the night, pushing and shoving, complaining to one another in the now too small nest under the eaves. But now they have gone and it is quiet without them. It seems strange to think of them skimming over the river Nile or doing aerobatics around the Great Pyramid.

But the swallows, like some of life's opportunities, have gone! One of these days I am going to get around to doing one of those things that I've been meaning to do for a long time: print out a big banner and fasten it along my office wall. The words will be, 'PEOPLE ARE MORE IMPORTANT THAN THINGS'. I think that the first time in my life that these words became meaningful for me was when my wife and I attended a camping rally in the north of England some years ago with a big crowd of fellow Christians. It was May time and the days were gloriously warm. But the nights were freezing. We froze, along with our hot water bottles, in our tent. We had travelled from Yorkshire to the rally in our brown Volkswagen van. It was really for carrying passengers, not a camper-van, but it had long seats that you could sleep on if necessary, and was warmer than a tent. We had also taken two girls from the church youth group along with us. They, too, had a flimsy tent and inadequate sleeping bags. They also froze at night. But I would not allow them to sleep in the van!

Looking back, it seems such a selfish attitude to take, but I was proud of that van, had done a lot of work on it, and I did not want it getting 'messed up'. I still feel ashamed when I look back to that incident. I hope that I have learned the lesson. As you read this, and perhaps apply it to your own life, for 'van' read 'house' or 'other possessions'. People really do matter more than 'things', whatever they may be. Sometimes, even for Christians, love of things may be stronger than love of those round about us for whom we have opportunities to do good, at the cost of our possessions and time, which are only temporary!

It was like that for a woman we read about in Mark's gospel, wasn't it? She had a wonderful 'thing', an alabaster bottle or flask of precious spikenard ointment. Perhaps it was the most precious possession she had. But there was a Person before her who was worth more than all the spikenard in the world. It was the Lord Jesus, and the time of His death and burial was drawing near. Her window of opportunity was very short; soon He would be gone, and her chance to use the ointment to show her love and appreciation of what He meant to her would be over.

We read that she broke her flask and poured out the precious ointment onto the head of the Lord Jesus (1). It was not wasted, despite the narrow thinking of some of the bystanders whose appreciation of Jesus and His worth fell far short of this woman's. She had taken her chance, she had done what she could, and her Lord's words are a continuing rebuke to those who prize their possessions (or their time) to such an extent that people for whom they could do good are neglected.

"Let her alone; why do you bother her? She has done a good work for Me. For you have the poor with you always, and whenever you wish you may do them good; but me you do not have always. She has done what she could; she has come beforehand to anoint My body for burial" (2). Opportunities to show love and kindness to parents, friends, neighbours, colleagues and school mates are for a limited time only. One morning you and I will wake up and they, like the swallows in autumn, will have gone. Therefore, let us take note of the exhortation written by Paul in the Bible, "Therefore, while we have opportunity, let us do good to all, especially to those who are of the household of faith" (3). Remember the swallows!

References: (1) Mk.14:3 (2) Mk.14:6-8 (3) Gal.6:10

18: UPSIDE-DOWN VALUES – THE POOR IN SPIRIT

How wonderful that our God should want to bless His creatures! In Genesis 1:28, God blessed the man and the woman that He had formed in His own image. He has not changed in His desires because, as the apostle John reminds us, "God is love" (1).

To bestow blessings on the earth and on its inhabitants was in the divine plan for mankind from the beginning. "The blessing of the Lord makes rich, and he adds no sorrow with it" (2). How sad that so much blessing was lost when Adam sinned. Adam's fallen race has been afflicted with the consequences of one man's disobedience from that day until this (3). But thank God that another Man has appeared to put things right and to restore the blessings of heaven.

In Matthew chapter 5 we have what is sometimes called 'The Sermon on the Mount', beginning with the 'beatitudes' meaning 'blessings'. The Greek word translated 'blessed' means to be fortunate, well off, counted happy. It was a happy day when great multitudes came together to listen to life-giving words from the mouth of God incarnate. Perhaps some were only there that day for the hoped-for physical blessings: healing of bodies and minds and perhaps another miraculously provided meal of bread and fishes. But that day the table was being set with food of a spiritual nature, food that is still available!

But what was the nature of the blessings that Jesus spoke about? Come with me please on a journey. Our destination is Bethlehem. Here we are in Manger Square, and in front of the Church of the Nativity, reputedly built over the birthplace of Israel's Messiah. Let's enter! Its low, isn't it? Mind your head! This door, the only entrance into the cavernous interior, is called the Door of Humility, so-called because everyone who wants to enter needs to bend low. The medieval crusader or the proud conqueror will not ride mounted in here; and even the common tourist has to bend!

And that serves as an illustration for this, the first of the beatitudes. It indicates that the way to experience the blessings of the kingdom is reserved not for everyone, but for those who are 'poor in spirit'. The same characteristics of the persons these blessings are offered to are clearly described by God in the words of the prophet Isaiah: "But this is the one to whom I will look: He who is humble and contrite in spirit and trembles at my word" (4).

These are the poor in spirit. Biblical history could fill a gallery with their portraits, men and women who deeply felt their own unworthiness before a holy God. Let's stop for a moment in front of Peter's portrait. Here he is out fishing on a boat on Galilee (5). He has fished all night with his companions and caught nothing. Now Jesus instructs him to cast his net on the other side. Skeptical, but willing to obey, Peter lowers the net. Now look at the huge catch that almost breaks the net! Wait, Peter is getting down at the feet of the Lord Jesus, recognising that he is in the presence of holiness, of deity. He confesses, "Depart from me, for I am a sinful man, O Lord" (6).

He is indeed a sinful man, always was, but now he recognises it, as someone convicted by the Spirit of God, and so qualified to be blessed by the God he is beginning to know personally. This incident and others, especially when he denied the Lord three times, would always, throughout Peter's life as a disciple of the Lord Jesus, be a reality check as to the nature of the pit from which he had been lifted (7) to be the recipient of the divine blessings for which he was so totally unworthy.

Only the King of Heaven could speak with authority about the 'kingdom of heaven'. The values of this new kingdom are indeed upside down, for it is the convicted who are converted, those who die who live, those who weep who laugh, those who mourn who dance, those who are first torn who are graciously made whole, and those who are poor who are rich!

References (all Scripture references are from the ESV): (1) 1 Jn.4:8 (2) Prov.10:22 (3) Rom.5:19 (4) Is.66:2 (5) Lk.5 (6) v.8 (7) Is.38:17

19: SPIRITUAL SECURITY

Imagine your computer linked to the Internet. Out there, in cyberspace, there are a whole host of potential enemies - viruses that have the ability to infect and render computer programmes useless. It's foolish to ignore the need for some security loaded on to protect against this threat, and to neglect to keep that security updated as the threat changes. A whole industry has arisen to provide internet security in this computer age. A 'Newsweek' article described the greatest potential threat to Britain's national security in the 21st century as being 'cyber warfare' (1).

Now think about a Christian having no security against the threat posed by a host of wicked beings, led by Satan, who, like viruses, are on the look-out for vulnerable targets. But God, in His wisdom and goodness, has supplied us with a 'security system', described in Ephesians 6, that is forever up-to-date. It just needs to be in place and operating!

First, there is the 'belt of truth' which needs to be fastened on. Then there is the 'breastplate of righteousness'. What is put into our hearts will come out in our lives. Jesus taught that it is out of the heart that evil thoughts come (2), and evil thoughts lead on to evil deeds. Visual images make up an important part of the weapons of mass destruction in the control of that evil adversary,

Satan. Right in the beginning Eve was tempted by what she saw, for the forbidden fruit was a 'delight to the eyes' (3). If we are actively living a holy life, protecting our eyes, being careful of what goes into our minds, putting to death the things of the flesh, then that part of the security is working, and our hearts are safe. In this computer age, unwholesome things like pornography are too easily accessible at the click of a button. If in this area we feel that we have already suffered defeat, the way back is via the cross and confession and taking God at His word (4).

In this battle we need to be constantly ready for action, for rapid response. Well-fitting shoes are essential and we need to be prepared at all times to give an answer to those who question or attack our faith (5). Knowledge of the Word of God is of paramount importance, or we will be easily knocked off course.

There is something that God has given to us which has to be taken up and used. That is faith, and it forms a shield. The Roman soldier's shield was large, protecting the whole body from fiery darts. God's Word says that 'we walk by faith, not by sight' (6) and that "without faith it is impossible to please him" (God) (7). Trusting that what has been revealed to us in God's Word is true, shows that the shield is being used. Fiery darts thrown by our enemies come in many forms, whether from unbelieving scientists, from militant atheists, or just from mockers, but faith will render their weapons ineffective.

Then there is the "helmet of salvation" and the "sword of the Spirit, which is the word of God" (8). Our minds are being bombarded all the time, and we need to be able to discern correctly what is of God and what is of the Devil. The Devil is more interested in us being fully occupied with temporal things - getting, spending and losing. A sword can be used for attack as well as for defence, and attack is often the best form of defence. We should not be afraid of quoting God's Word, sometimes just to ourselves, whenever we find ourselves in a situation where we are being pressured to conform to this world and its standards.

The question of whether we need to upgrade our spiritual protection to a 'current' version is easily answered. No! The original armour, supplied by God and described by Paul in Ephesians 6, is never out of date. Each piece is vital and must be put on daily, with prayer in the Spirit. Sometimes we may have a need to press the 'refresh' button; our lives for Christ and our rewards at the judgement seat of Christ are at stake!

References (all Scripture references from the ESV): (1) Underhill, W. Newsweek, 20 October 2010 (2) See Matt.15:19 (3) Gen.3:6 (4) 1 Jn.1:9 (5) Col.4:6; 1 Pet.3:15 (6) 2 Cor.5:7 (7) Heb.11:6 (8) Eph.6:17

20: FIRE! FIRE!

The man was a smoker. Caught in the hospital corridor by the sister of the ward where he was a patient, he hastily looked for somewhere to dispose of his cigarette. Ah, a chute in the wall! In went the cigarette, still smouldering. Down to the basement it fell, into a linen skip. Soon the skip was ablaze. The fire spread upward, out of control. Before long the whole hospital tower block was engulfed in flames and smoke. Desperate staff tried to evacuate helpless patients trapped on the upper storeys. Many sick, frail, elderly patients, the bed-bound and children had no chance to escape.

Frightening? The above description is fiction, but very realistic, from a film shown some years ago to hospital staff in one part of the UK to alert them to the danger of fire in their work environment.

Fire is to be feared!
Fire in the Scriptures is used to describe the eventual experience of the unsaved. It is the Lord Jesus who will one day say, "Depart from me, you cursed, into the eternal fire prepared for the devil and his angels" (1). In Revelation 20 the lake of fire is described graphically as being the ultimate, eternal destiny of the Devil. How thankful we should be that as believers we are saved by the grace of our God from eternal fire.

Fire cleanses!

When the Lord Jesus entered the Temple courts in Jerusalem to cleanse God's house of the market traders and money changers (2), He was, in character, 'refiner's fire' (3). He was eaten up with zeal for the holiness of God's house. It was meant to be a holy place, in keeping with God's nature. Men had defiled it. The Lord Jesus swept them away with divine and yet compassionate majesty, (for He did not overturn the tables on which the doves were sold) and vindicated the holiness of His God and Father.

Fire consumes!

On a wet and windy Sunday morning in Belfast, Northern Ireland, many years ago, an incident happened on the way home from attending church that forever changed the life of a young local girl. Moved by compassion to help a frail old lady carrying a heavy bundle along the street in the wind and rain, and feeling very embarrassed in front of lots of 'respectable' Christians, just as they were passing a drinking fountain at the road-side, some verses of Scripture suddenly flashed into Amy Carmichael's mind: "Gold, silver, precious stones, wood, hay, stubble; every man's work shall be made manifest; for the day shall declare it, because it shall be revealed by fire; and the fire shall try every man's work of what sort it is. If any man's work abide…" (4).

The experience was so real that Amy turned to see who was speaking to her. Recalling the incident, she writes years later, 'I turned to see the voice that spoke with me. The fountain, the muddy street, the people with their politely surprised faces, all this I saw, but saw nothing else. The blinding flash had come and gone; the ordinary was all about us. We went on. I said nothing to anyone, but I knew that something had happened that had changed life's values. Nothing could ever matter again but the things that are eternal' (5).

From that point on Amy sought to serve the One who had done so much for her and eventually God led her to India where she spent the rest of her life in loving service, rescuing young people from moral danger and making a home for them where her Lord and Saviour who be pre-eminent in every aspect of life.

Amy Carmichael had realised that at the judgement seat of Christ our works as believers are going to be assessed. Only the works that survive the consuming fire will remain, worthy of being rewarded. Should that not cause each one of us to search our hearts and test the motives for all that we do and to examine our lives to see what we are spending our time doing?

> Only one life, 'twill soon be past,
> Only what's done for Christ will last. (6)

Fire shines!

The Lord Jesus described John the Baptist as "a burning and a shining lamp" (7). Through his preaching, the hearts of many were laid bare and lives were changed. John shone powerfully for God in a sinful and needy generation! How we, too, as believers should long to be rekindled in our love for the living God, and earnestly desire a deeper experience of Him, whose eyes are described in Revelation as being 'a flame of fire' (8).

> Give me the love that leads the way,
> The faith that nothing can dismay,
> The hope no disappointments tire,
> The passion that will burn like fire,

> Let me not sink to be a clod;
> Make me Thy fuel, Flame of God. (9)
> (Amy Carmichael)

References (all Scripture references from the ESV, unless otherwise stated): (1) Matt.25:41 (2) Jn.2:13-17 (3) Mal.3:2 (4) 1 Cor.3:12-14, KJV (5) Frank Houghton, Amy Carmichael of Dohnavur (6) C.T. Studd, Only One Life (7) Jn.5:35 (8) Rev.1:14 (9) From "Towards Jerusalem"

21: THE FIRST KISS

The kiss of the lover

To be in love defies scientific explanation. But romantic love (Greek: 'eros') is something very real. Sometimes it is love at first sight; at other times it develops slowly. However, it arises, love is a living thing and is meant to grow, mature and develop. Young lovers may start by holding hands, before the poignant moment when the first kiss is exchanged. What tenderness, overflowing of affection and oneness of desire is being expressed and exchanged! You can only really know what being in love feels like if you have been in love yourself – like the writer of the 'Song of Songs': "Let him kiss me with the kisses of his mouth! For your love is better than wine…" (1).

It is God who has created the desire for two lovers to kiss each other. Our society is even degrading the romantic kiss, making it part of our throw-away culture where casual relationships with routine kissing are no more than a desire for personal gratification. But for the one who waits for true love, then the kiss has special significance – a bond that two hearts are united in love; a precursor of so many more physical expressions of love, ordained of God, that will naturally follow in time, as that love is consummated within the divinely created framework of marriage. Surely this is something worth waiting for.

The reconciling kiss

Psalm 2:12 says: "Kiss the Son, lest he be angry, and you perish in the way, for his wrath is quickly kindled. Blessed are all who take refuge in him." This unusual verse reminds us that sinners need to be reconciled to God through His Son, otherwise they will experience His wrath against sin and suffer the judgement that their sins deserve. This reconciliation is only made possible because "Christ also suffered once for sins, the righteous for the unrighteous, that he might bring us to God" (2).

Perhaps the coming to Jesus in faith is seen, symbolically, as kissing Him, because it indicates a right relationship has been established with God on a personal level. It is a kiss bringing peace. "Therefore, since we have been justified by faith, we have peace with God through our Lord Jesus Christ" (3).

The holy kiss

Why did the first Christians greet each other with a holy kiss, probably on the cheek (4)? Was it a sign that the peace and love that had been established between God in heaven and men on earth through the work of the Son was now also being evidenced between followers of Christ on earth? A kiss, something personal, something pure, something that spoke of reconciliation, love and unity, found its expression within the constitution and practices of a new people of God founded upon new covenant truths, expressing the inexpressible and abiding love of God.

The kiss of betrayal

I wonder when was the first time Judas kissed Jesus? In the Garden of Gethsemane, it was a kiss indicating treachery in Judas' heart, for he was betraying his Lord and Master (5). How more corrupt could the meaning of a kiss have become than when it was used as a sign that Jesus was the one whom the armed guards were to arrest and lead away to suffer and die! God was graciously allowing something that was ordained for good (a kiss) to be used by evil to bring about His purposes of love towards those who, by nature, were His enemies.

While some may experience true romantic love on earth, earthly and transient, emotional experiences will be far exceeded by the spiritual realities of heaven when we will be with the One who created human emotions and who is Himself love in all its fullness and completeness. Let us treasure in our hearts that first kiss with the One who loved us and gave Himself for us that we may be forever with Him, close to His heart.

> Loved with everlasting love,
> Led by grace that love to know;
> Spirit, breathing from above,
> Thou hast taught me it is so.
> Oh, this full and perfect peace!
> Oh, this transport all divine!
> In a love which cannot cease,
> I am His, and He is mine.
> (G.W. Robinson)

References (all Scripture references from the ESV: (1) Songs 1:2 (2) 1 Pet.3:18 (3) Rom.5:1 (4) 1 Cor.16:20 (5) Lk.22:48

22: TWITCHING

My brother, a bird-watcher (or 'twitcher'), was excited. We had brought him out on a two-day trip to Donegal on the west coast of Ireland. Having found a hostel to stay in, we set off to explore the area with its wild rocky fells, high cliffs, deserted beaches and Atlantic breakers. With nothing between us and America except water, we set off to walk along the beach.

While his binoculars were trained on two large black birds feeding on the cliff-side grass which he identified as being a rare species and which caused him great excitement (he was twitching all over!), my attention was drawn to a flock of sheep which were also grazing on the grassy slopes that tumbled down to the beach. They were on the move. I spotted the shepherd before I saw his dogs. There were two of them, black and white collies, working hard, perfectly coordinated, running this way, pausing, lying down, running back the other way, skilfully coercing the sheep in the required direction and collecting up any strays. The shepherd's shouts and whistles gave the dogs their orders, and these, obviously well-trained, responded to their master's voice. This was a beauty to behold in their perfect obedience.

Their master's voice! There was a time when THE Master's voice was heard in this world, sometimes loud and authoritative, saying, "Peace, be still!" (1) quietening the raging sea; sometimes gently and lovingly saying, "Come to Me" (2). What a privilege to listen to Jesus' voice and converse with Him face to face! The incarnate Word was revealing the heart and mind of the invisible God. There were times for questions – there's nothing wrong with questions as they can reveal a healthy, inquisitive mind. But there were other times when, the Bible says, "from that day on no one dared to ask him any more questions" (3). Yes, there is "a time to keep silence, and a time to speak" (4).

Healthy asking must turn to quietly trusting. There are some things that our Master speaks to us about that we will never understand fully down here – things which "we see in a mirror, dimly" (5). Then it is a time for resting on faith. After all, we don't see the whole picture down here and some knowledge is too deep for us; such as how and where the Good Shepherd is leading His sheep, going on ahead, calling, not driving with dogs. At times all we hear Him say is, "Follow Me" (6). He will not take us where He will not go Himself. "I am with you always" (7). So we...

> Trust and obey, for there's no other way
> To be happy in Jesus, but to trust and obey. (8)

I felt led that day on the beach in Donegal to bend down and write something in the sand with a stick before we left the seashore and climbed the 167 steps to the cliff top and went on our way. What did I write? 'JESUS IS LORD'. And He is. Lord of the sand, sea, cliffs, rare birds, sheep, men and women, boys and girls; Lord of all. The Atlantic breakers came in later that day and washed away that truth written in the sand, but one day the Master's voice will be heard again on earth and at His name every knee will bow, and every tongue will confess that Jesus Christ is Lord, to the glory of God the Father (9). That truth will never be erased for the whole of eternity. Now that really is something to start 'twitching' about!

References: (1) Mk.4:39 (2) Matt.11:28 (3) Matt.22:46 NIV (4) Eccl.3:7 (5) 1 Cor.13:12 (6) e.g. Matt.4:19 (7) Matt.28:20 (8) John H. Sammis (9) Phil.2:10-11

23: UNSOUGHT

A couple of years ago I happened to be passing along a road and over the wall was a field that had a stream running through it, with quite a steep bank down to the water from the level field. In the field were a neighbour's sheep with their lambs. One lamb had wandered away down the bank to the water's edge and seemed to be having difficulty getting back up. It was making a lot of noise. I didn't think too much about it as I walked on. Surely the lamb would eventually find a way up to rejoin its mother, or the farmer would spot the distressed lamb as he was checking his flock. A few days later I passed that way again and, being reminded of the lamb, I stopped and looked over the wall. The dead body of the lamb lay in the cold water. Rescue had never come.

In her autobiography (1), Patricia St. John, the author of so many books that have thrilled, challenged and taught children (and adults) over the years, and who writes from her own life experiences and missionary work in North Africa, includes a chapter about the Mission Hospital at Tangier in Morocco. She writes of the extreme difficulties of bringing the message of the gospel to the people of that Muslim land and of the work of the hospital in opening hearts through the provision of free medical help to the needy at a time when no other help was available.

She writes of the day that a poor, ill Moorish child was brought into the hospital in the arms of her father from a distant tribal village. Nothing could be done for her, and she was taken out of the hospital by her father to an animals' hut (a fundak) to die in his arms – the only one she knows who loves her. This is her poem:

FATIMA

'I will die in my father's arms' she said,
'Amid scenes and faces I know,
Where donkeys stamp in the Fundak yard
Where straw is scanty and the cobbles are hard,
And the vermined squatters cook on the shard,
'Tis there that I long to go.'

'Not among faces foreign and kind
Would I plunge to the straits of death,
But under heavens starry and free
In the well-known haunts of poverty,
Held to the heart that yearns for me
Would I yield up my rattling breath.'

And through broken speech shall the Questing Love
Surge to her last alarms,
That scorns no channel to heal and bless,
Unperceived, through man's gentleness;
She shall rest in her final helplessness
In the Everlasting Arms.

Loving, unloved; seeking, unsought;
Knowing, the while unknown;
Denied all access, pursuing His quest,

> The tide steals in on her long unrest:
> Through the peace of a father's ragged breast
> He shall gather and bear His own.

So writes Patricia St John of this little lost lamb. Fatima finally dies in the arms of her poverty-stricken earthly father who loved her, but unseen, behind and underneath are the 'everlasting arms' of the Good Shepherd, for, "he will gather the lambs in his arms" (2).

It is strange how the Spirit of God can take a single word out of a poem, give it a different emphasis, and bring home a deep challenge to the heart of the reader. That's how it was for me. 'Unsought' was the word. As a missionary, Patricia St John carried the message of the good news of a shepherd who laid down His life for the sheep to a people whose hearts were as stony as their land. Jesus loved, but few loved Him in return. He came, seeking those who were lost, but few were seeking Him. He was unsought, but He never stopped loving and seeking.

And then the sadness came to my heart, along with the challenge: what of the lambs and sheep who are on the point of perishing today; men, women, boys and girls like the lamb in the neighbour's field that no-one cared enough about to save? Who will go to them and tell them of a loving Saviour? Is there no one willing to leave the 'ninety-nine' and go and look for the one who is lost? Another lover of souls, and especially the souls of little lost lambs, wrote,

> O for a passionate passion for souls,
> O for a pity that yearns!
> O for a love that loves unto death,

O for a fire that burns! (3)

References (all Scripture references from the ESV): (1) Patricia St John Tells Her Own Story, OM Publishing, 1993 (2) Isaiah 40:11 (3) Amy Carmichael, founder of the Dohnavur Fellowship in S. India which provided a home for little children, especially girls saved from a life of deified sin in the Hindu Temples.

24: A REALITY CHECK

Going to a fitness program for the first time certainly gives you a reality check! Especially if the instructor puts you on a piece of apparatus that measures your heart function while you are exercising! For those of us who get out of breath climbing the stairs when going to bed, it can come as a bit of a shock to realise why this should be so. It certainly focuses the mind to realise the truth of the scripture that says, "our outer self is wasting away…" (1).

The Apostle also, when referring to this body that is sown into the ground at death, says that it is 'sown in weakness' (2) and further on in the same chapter describes our bodies as 'perishable' (3). And yet, sometimes, especially if we are young, we live as if we are going to be around down here forever.

The divine diagnosis that we are weak, wasting away and perishing, certainly focuses the mind. You begin to ask yourself the question, "Now what is there important to get done while I'm still around?" The "things to do" lists start getting re-evaluated! "All the world's a stage." That's what Shakespeare wrote, anyway; "and all the men and women merely players" (4). Well, I don't think it's quite like that. Things that happen down here have eternal significance for each individual. We're not 'merely players' and it's not all over once the curtain comes down. But I think I know what Shakespeare was getting at. I believe the wise preacher expressed it very clearly in Ecclesiastes: "Vanity of vanities, says the Preacher, vanity of vanities! All is vanity. What does man gain by all the toil at which he toils under the sun? A generation goes, and a generation comes, but the earth remains forever" (5).

Years ago, when at college, my friend Davy and I were co-opted (I can't remember volunteering!) to stage manage a number of the college productions, both plays and musicals. I remember one set that we worked on together. There were a number of different scene changes that required some ingenuity in design so that the changes could be made swiftly and efficiently. We worked hard on that set; in fact, we used more screws than nails! The end result was so well built that you could have actually lived in it. The trouble was, it was for a PLAY! The whole production was over in three days, and then everything was ripped down.

You see, we had forgotten that what was required was only something temporary that would do the job but, at the same time, giving the audience the impression that it was a solid, permanent structure. With the effort we used we could have been better employed by the local building contractors in town! A least what we had built would have been useful for longer than three days!

When we come up against the stark fact that life down here in this body is definitely not 'everlasting', we start asking ourselves the question, "Well, what am I doing to get ready for the world to come? What is it that I am building down here? Am I using screws instead of nails, as if I'm going to be living here forever, rather than accepting that what I'm living in, no matter how many times I go to the gym, is just temporary accommodation with a limited life-span?"

So, what is the conclusion to all this? It's the same conclusion that the Preacher came to at the end of his book: "The end of the matter; all has been heard. Fear God and keep his commandments, for this is the whole duty of man. For God will bring every deed into judgement, with every secret thing, whether good or evil" (6).

Life is precious, and no doubt I will be working a little harder in the fitness suite, trying to keep going as long as possible, like the rest of us! But I want also to keep my eyes on the sequel to this little time down here, knowing that when this scene changes, and the temporal props are taken away, the final eternal scene which God has built will last forever! "So we do not lose heart. Though our outer self is wasting away, our inner self is being renewed day by day. For this light momentary affliction is preparing for us an eternal weight of glory beyond all comparison, as we look not to the things that are seen but to the things that are unseen. For the things that are seen are transient, but the things that are unseen are eternal" (7).

References (all Scripture references from the ESV): (1) 2 Cor.4:16 (2) 1 Cor.15:43 (3) 1 Cor.15:50,53-54 (4) William Shakespeare, As You Like It, Act 2, Scene 4 (5) Eccl.1:2-4 (6) Eccl.12:13-14 (7) 2 Cor.4:16-18

25: BETRAYED!

Although nothing could ever surprise the Lord Jesus Christ – for His divine omniscience meant He knew the end from the beginning – still, in His experience of manhood, He knew what it was to be deeply hurt. The prophet Isaiah wrote that the Messiah would be a "man of sorrows" (1). His pain would not only be physical, but spiritual and also emotional.

What causes deeper emotional pain than to be betrayed? The Lord Jesus was not just betrayed by an enemy, but by someone who was very close to Him – a friend and a companion. David, writing by the Spirit in the Psalms, expressed the experience of the Lord: "Even my close friend in whom I trusted, who ate my bread, has lifted his heel against me" (2). These prophetic words were quoted to Jesus' disciples by the Lord in the upper room on the night that they were being fulfilled (3). What sorrow and hurt He must have felt!

'Betrayed' is the title of a book written by Stan Telchin (4). It describes Stan's experience when his daughter phoned him one day to say that she had accepted Jesus as her Messiah and had become a Christian. He felt betrayed! How could his daughter, whom he loved, do such a thing? Stan was Jewish. He resolutely set out to prove her mistaken and misguided. Being a methodical man, he collected his resource material and began reading the New Testament for himself. He planned to find 'ammunition' to convince his daughter that she was wrong and to persuade her to return to the Jewish faith. Love for her, and a desire to rescue her from the 'clutches' of Christianity, spurred him on.

As Stan began to read the New Testament accounts of Jesus' life and ministry, and to compare them with the Old Testament prophecies concerning the coming Messiah, Stan began a journey into faith. He describes in his book his initial deep hurt and sense of betrayal and then his final joy at his own discovery and acceptance of Jesus as Messiah and personal Saviour and Lord.

The final chapter of Jesus' sojourn on earth as a man of sorrows began that fateful night when Judas appeared with a band of armed officers to arrest Jesus at the Garden of Gethsemane. Matthew records the depth of Judas' treachery: "Now the betrayer had given them a sign, saying, 'The one I kiss is the man; seize him.' And he came up to Jesus at once and said, 'Greetings, Rabbi!' And he kissed him. Jesus said to him, 'Friend, do what you came to do'" (5).

There was a deep wound inflicted that night, deeper than any Roman nail or spear: betrayed with a kiss by one whom Jesus called 'friend'. Jesus had selected Judas to be one of His twelve divinely chosen men who would follow Him, learn from Him, be sent out by Him with special powers to heal and cast out evil spirits (6) and to be His witnesses. Judas had a privileged place in Jesus' inner circle. Luke, in his account of the choosing of the Twelve after Jesus had spent the night in prayer, ends his list with the words, "and Judas Iscariot, who became a traitor" (7). While the other disciples were learning to become fishers of men, Judas was learning treachery.

John, in his gospel account, gives us a further insight into the character of Judas. Mary of Bethany had used expensive ointment to anoint Jesus in an act of loving devotion, and Judas criticised her actions, saying that the ointment could have been sold and the money given to the poor. John writes: "He said this, not because he cared about the poor, but because he was a thief, and having charge of the moneybag he used to help himself to what was put into it" (8). This love of money showed a flaw in Judas' character that motivated him to go to the high priests and agree to betray Jesus for thirty pieces of silver.

It is also recorded by John concerning Judas, that during the meal in the upper room, "Satan entered into him" (9). Treachery, betrayal, greed and Satan – they form an evil quartet. The kind and manner of betrayal Jesus experienced was unique to Him. Christians have sometimes experienced betrayal by someone they trusted, and found it to be a very bitter experience. Sometimes, sadly, it is a fellow Christian who lets us down in a time of need, and it can be a struggle to pray for those whom we feel have hurt us and to be willing to forgive them. If that is your experience just now, then there is One who can sympathise with you, and who ever lives to help you and to intercede for you, for He is a great high priest (10).

References (all Scripture references from the ESV): (1) Is.53:3 (2) Ps.41:9 (3) Jn.13:18 (4) Stan Telchin, Betrayed, Marshalls, 1981 (5) Matt.26:48-50 (6) Matt.10:1,8 (7) Lk.6:16 (8) Jn.12:6 (9) Jn.13:27 (10) Heb.7:25-26

26: NO CUTBACKS

"I have called this special meeting of all staff because of an emergency that has arisen," said the Matron of the small hospice (1) in the north of England where I was working some years ago. "We are running short of funds and, because of the recession, charitable giving on which this hospice depends has considerably reduced. The trustees of the hospice are being forced to make cutbacks in expenditure to enable us to remain open and to serve this community. If any members of staff have any suggestions on how we can save money, please speak up!"

"Matron, I have a suggestion to make," said one nurse. "Our stock of china cups and saucers that we use to serve tea to the patients is getting low because of constant breakages. Could we not just use disposable plastic cups instead of the more expensive china cups?"

The Matron thought for a while, and then replied, "Although it seems a small matter, I believe that the quality of the china cups that we use for our patients is very important. By serving tea in the best cups, we are making an unspoken statement about how we view them and what worth we are putting on them. We are saying that they are worth so much that we are willing to use expensive china cups rather than cheaper plastic disposable ones. We are saying that, in the few weeks that they have left on this earth, they are valuable and cared for, no matter what their social status in life or their intellectual ability and achievements, and no matter what it costs us. Although we will have to make cutbacks in other areas of expenditure, this is one area we must protect."

Do you think that Matron had a point? As I look back on this incident in my own experience, a few thoughts come into my own mind which are connected to it. First, God gave His very best for us. In sending Jesus into this world, God paid a very high price – the highest He could pay. At the same time, He made a statement about how He views us, how much He values us. There were to be no cutbacks in the measure of the love that God was expending to redeem us back to Him. 'God is love' (2), and what He gave is the very best that Love could give, as reflected in the words of Graham Kendrick:

> Such love springs from eternity.
> Such love, streaming through history.
> Such love, fountain of life to me.
> O Jesus, such love.

It also calls us to consider the response that we are making to our God "who did not spare his own Son but gave him up for us all" (3). Mary came with her alabaster jar of precious ointment to break open and pour on the Lord Jesus, and the Lord recognised how much Mary valued Him (4). "What can I give Him, poor as I am?" asks the writer of the old Christmas carol, and gives the only worthy answer, "…give my heart" (5).

We have a number of hand-crafted articles about the house which are each unique in some way, like a fruit bowl made by a local wood-turner, hand-knitted woollen garments and an embroidered tablecloth. Each item has been made with care. There is a prophecy made by Isaiah concerning those for whom the Lord has paid such a high price and who are the workmanship of His own hands. It says, "He shall see of the travail of His soul and shall be satisfied" (6). We are God's workmanship (7) and that fact first of all gives Him pleasure as, throughout all eternity, He sees and enjoys the results of His own carefully finished work which caused Him such trouble in His soul. But He also made us to be used, having prepared good works for us to walk in and not just to sit idly on a shelf!

Very importantly, like the terminally ill patients in the hospice who drank tea out of the best china cups, we are given a personal awareness of the worth with which we are regarded by the One who never will make any cutbacks in our care – neither in time nor in eternity.

References (all Scripture references from the ESV, unless stated otherwise): (1) A hospice is a place where terminally ill patients are looked after until their death (2) 1 Jn.4:8 (3) Rom.8:32 (4) Jn.12:3 (5) 'In the bleak mid-winter', Christina Rossetti (1830-1894) (6) Is.53:11 RV (7) See Eph.2:10

27: TO THE SCRAPHEAP!

"To the scrapheap!" That's what I occasionally have to say when I open the kiln door and remove the pots that have just completed their ten-hour firing process. Taking out the jugs, bowls and mugs, one by one and examining them closely sometimes reveals that cracks have developed or a glaze has run or that the intense heat (1100 degrees Celsius) has caused the pot to blister. So to the scrap heap outside the pottery door it goes! Thankfully, not many end up this way, for a lot of time and energy has been expended on moulding, decorating and firing each pot. Paul, writing to the saints at Corinth, reminds them that they, or at least their bodies, are "jars of clay" (1). What was true for them is also true for us; we are physically composed of "dust from the ground" (2) like Adam. Our bodies deteriorate with time, get old and weak, develop serious physical ailments, show evidence of unavoidable mental aging and are prone to the effects of our inherited fallen, sinful nature. At death, our bodies return to dust (3)!

But, praise God that, for Christians, these bodies contain a 'treasure'! And this treasure will never decay or perish. It is our spiritual life, given as a gift from God, and it's His life – the life of our Lord Jesus. He lives in the believer (4)! That is the most amazing truth about the Christian life, and because of it we shall never, ever, end up on the 'scrapheap'. Jesus said, "I give them eternal life, and they will never perish" (5). Sadly, we do fail at times. Our love waxes and wanes – it goes up and down like a temperature chart at the end of the hospital bed. If our salvation depended upon ourselves, we would soon be rejects. But we are reminded that "he who began a good work in you will bring it to completion at the day of Jesus Christ" (6). He is the potter – the Master Potter – and we are the clay. He suffered the intense heat of His Calvary experience on our account, and He won't fail to finish His work. Isaiah's prophecy reminds us that "He shall see of the travail of His soul, and shall be satisfied" (7).

One future day, He will see the results of His finished work; there won't be any mistakes on His part, (though we ourselves could lose some of our rewards at the judgement seat of Christ when our lives of obedient service to Him as Lord are assessed). So take courage! You and I are living in jars of clay. We may suffer many knocks and bruises, afflictions, even persecutions because of our faith, experience mental and physical wear and tear, and maybe battle against chronic conditions day after day, or even have a terminal illness.

But, Paul writes, "…we do not lose heart. Though our outward self is wasting away, our inner self is being renewed day by day. For this light momentary affliction is preparing for us an eternal weight of glory beyond all comparison, as we look not to the things that are seen but to the things that are unseen. For the things that are seen are transient, but the things that are unseen are eternal" (8).

References: (1) 2 Cor.4:7 (2) Gen.2:7 (3) Gen.3:19 (4) 2 Cor.4:6-11; Col.1:27 (5) Jn.10:28 (6) Phil.1:6 (7) Is.53:11 RV (8) 2 Cor.4:16-18

28: NOBBUT CLAY!

Soil Hill, situated a few miles outside Halifax towards Keighley, between the A644 and the A629, was the site of the last of the Halifax country potteries producing "crocks" from local materials. Earthenware clay was dug from the hillside and turned on the wheel into mixing bowls, stew pots, chicken and hen feeders, rhubarb forcers, plant pots, strawberry pots, and a host of other things.

The last potter to work at Soil Hill was called Isaac Button. He was a skilled craftsman who dug the clay by hand, operated the blunger and sieve, put the clay through the pugging mill, wedged the clay, threw the pots on the wheel amazingly quickly, fired the kiln with best coal, and then sold his produce around the area to meet the needs of the kitchen and the dairy.

Though regarding himself as a humble workman, Isaac Button became well known to other craft potters around the world, and admired for his craftsmanship. A film was made about his work, which you can find by searching his name on Youtube, and examples of the pots that Isaac made at Soil Hill can be seen in Bankfield Museum, Halifax, West Yorkshire, and in homes around the area.

Isaac couldn't understand why so much fuss was made about what he considered to be simple earthenware pots, which were not works of art in his eyes. "They're nobbut clay," he was once heard to remark! ("Nobbut" is "nothing but" in Yorkshire slang!)

"Nobbut clay"! That's true of ourselves too, isn't it? We are just made from the dust of the earth and to dust we shall return, as the Bible reminds us. However, God wants to do something special for us and with us; He wants us to become containers for a TREASURE given by Him! God wants to shine His light into our hearts. This happens when we are saved and God's Spirit comes to live within us!

Paul, the Apostle, writing to fellow Christians in Corinth, describes what happened to him on the Damascus road, to those in Corinth when they first believed the gospel, and to all 'born again' believers everywhere then and now, in the following words: "For God, who said, "Let light shine out of darkness," has shone in our hearts to give the light of the knowledge of the glory of God in the face of Jesus Christ. But we have this treasure in jars of clay to show that the surpassing power belongs to God and not to us" (1).

"Treasure in jars of clay" – that's our clay bodies, and God put the treasure there! It's an everlasting treasure which will never wear out or become out of date. It is the "free gift of God" which is "eternal life" and it is "in Christ Jesus our Lord" (2). Only Jesus, the Son of God, paid the price to obtain it for us. We still live in our fragile clay bodies, often ending up in the doctor's surgery or Halifax Royal Hospital for treatment! But Christians have a treasure inside that will never perish, and one day God will give us a new body to match what He has put inside.

Soil Hill pottery is abandoned and derelict, having closed in the 1960's. A few older local people will still remember Isaac Button the last potter, with his pipe in his mouth! The old industries go, the world changes, but "Jesus Christ is the same yesterday, and today and forever" (3). Are you "Nobbut clay?"

Yes, but special to God. He sent His Son to die so that He could shine light into your heart, into your jar of clay. How? By repenting of sin, and putting your trust in the Son of God who loved you and gave Himself for you.

References: (1) 2 Cor.4:6-7 (2) Rom.6:23 (3) Heb.13:8.

29: UNDER MY NOSE!

Talking of pottery, (my hobby, as you will have guessed by now) some years ago an interest in the history of the pottery-making industry had led me onto a hillside a few miles outside Halifax. I was searching for the remains of a long disused pottery site, but had reached a dead end! It was in the early 1970s. I had been down to the Buckley area in north Wales. Researching the development of the Buckley potteries, I discovered that over one hundred years ago a potter with the name "Catherall" had travelled north to Halifax. He had established a workshop and kiln somewhere near Halifax. I thought I would try and find the site.

This led me to the reference library in Halifax. On very old maps I located a number of sites in the hills around the area. Armed with an ordinance survey map, the day came when I set off to find the lost pottery founded by a Buckley potter. However, when I came to the precise spot where, according to the old maps, there should be the remains of a pottery site. I found nothing! As I leaned on a dry stone wall, one typical of the area, looking over at a small field and a farm house and barn in front of me on the remote hillside, I could see no signs of any past industry in that area. I had reached a dead end! Where could the old pottery have been situated?

As I leaned on the wall, I suddenly noticed something! The local stone used for the field walls was millstone grit, but the section of wall I was leaning on was of a different nature. I suddenly realised that the wall was built of rough black fire-bricks covered in slag, of the kind that had once been part of a kiln! Here was the very evidence I was looking for! It was under my nose all the time! As I looked more carefully at the field in front, I could see grass-covered circular mounds, places where clay had been prepared in pits. Evidence that this was indeed the lost site was all around. No doubt if I had started to dig into the field archaeological evidence would confirm it! And it had been under my nose all along! My search was over!

There came another day, some years later, when I was again searching for something. This time it was more personal. I was searching for peace! I was looking for answers to life's problems. I had become very pessimistic about the way the world is going. I had searched hard, trying to find answers. My search led me to Jerusalem in Israel in 1975.

The name 'Jerusalem' means 'City of Peace' and I thought I would find peace there. Perhaps believing in God would be the answer? I knew that I had broken God's commandments in the Bible and that I needed to be forgiven. All my attempts to find peace by my own efforts of cleaning up my life had only led to a dead end! That day in Jerusalem I reached the lowest point of my life, feeling utter despair!

Suddenly I realised something! The answer was in my own pocket, right under my nose! It had been there all the time, for I carried a little red Gideon's Bible with me that I had been given when I left school in Yorkshire, aged sixteen. In it I had read about God's laws which I knew I had broken; for example, God said "Thou shalt not steal", and I had stolen. There were other sins, too. But that day I realised that in that same Bible God had provided the answer, for it says that He sent His Son, the Lord Jesus Christ to deal with sin!

Jesus, the only sinless person, had lived a perfect life, and had then laid it down willingly on the cross as a sacrifice to cancel sin. God had accepted that sacrifice and therefore was able to offer forgiveness to 'lost sheep' like myself. Jesus had paid the price. Salvation was free - a gift! It was a wonderful discovery, for it brought me peace, a peace that has lasted from that day to this.

The answer was in my pocket, 'under my nose', all the time. Having repented (turned away from) my sins I accepted the Lord Jesus Christ as my Saviour that day. Many years have come and gone since then, but the salvation I received that November day in Jerusalem has not changed, because Jesus has not changed. God raised Him on the third day, and He lives in Heaven until He comes again for those who have accepted Him.

My Gideon's Bible says that: "Jesus Christ is the same yesterday, today, yea and forever". Check it out for yourself; it's in Hebrews 13:8 in the New Testament. Another verse says "Being justified by faith we have peace with God" (1). It brought me satisfaction to have discovered that lost pottery site outside Halifax that day, but the most important discovery of my life is that there is a God in Heaven who loves me and that His salvation is a gift, provided by grace, and received by faith. When I returned to England I was baptised by immersion in a little church hall (Waterloo Hall) in Halifax on June 19th, 1977 and became a follower of Jesus with others in a church of God. That was also another happy day, a day of saying 'thank you' to God for giving me peace.

References: (1) Rom.5:1

30: SEAMLESS

"Now the coat was without seam, woven from the top in one piece (1)."

"Will all passengers travelling to Belfast International airport on the 1510 flight please proceed to gate 2."

"What are our seat numbers, Sue?"

"Row 14, seats E and F."

"Oh no, we are directly over the wings. We won't be able to see much today."

"Let's ask the hostess if there are any seats free front or back."

"This is better, but it looks like we are in for a cloudy trip. Not much chance of looking down for familiar landmarks today!"

"Never mind. Let's just relax, read, and enjoy the flight."

That's how the journey started, after a long weekend away visiting friends in England. Sue was soon deeply engrossed in her Patricia St John book, being transported into a lost childhood world that the author writes about so vividly from her own experience. In some of her stories, children explore the unspoilt countryside without fear or danger, and learn unchanging spiritual lessons about, for example, the lost sheep and the good shepherd, and discover the love of God through the adventures they have in the less dangerous world of the early 1900's. Christian adults who missed out on Patricia St John books in their childhood have a lot of catching up to do! Flights on a cloudy day are a good opportunity!

Meanwhile I was being transported too. The vista I looked out on from the plane window was incomparably beautiful, like another country; so different from the one we had just left, murky in the industrial English midlands, under the January clouds. Up there the sun was shining in all its strength, and the clouds formed a rolling countryside as far as the eye could see. Observant air travellers will know what I mean. It was like flying over fields of snow and ice, and then there would be features such as gleaming mountains and distant valleys. It truly seemed to be a land in its own right, a place apart, so clean, clear, touched here and there with miniature rainbows that followed the plane, perfectly round as if they hovered over an unseen throne in a land untouched by human hand.

It was a place where you could find yourself saying "I believe in angels," for it seemed like their kind of country. In fact, it was a very heavenly place indeed, and the longer I looked out on it, the more I appreciated it, the more I wanted to stay up there and for the flight to go on and on for ever.

Was it a taste of Heaven? Heaven is after all a place, and it is where we Christians believe we are going and where the Lord is. "How", I asked myself, as I sat on the plane revelling in this glorious vista, "did we get here?!" We had taken off from East Midlands Airport, climbed skywards in the hands of a skilled pilot, spent a few minutes flying blind through wisps of misty cloud, with an occasional fleeting glance below of motorways, housing estates, football pitches and factories. And then the clouds were behind us and below us and above was ethereal blue and the sun shining as if it had always been shining with no such thing as night. From below to above, from one experience to another, from one land to another, had been achieved through a seamless experience, with no breaks, (like the Lord's coat taken by the soldiers at Calvary).

The one had been a continuation of the other, yet both so totally different from one another. It so illustrated for me our experience in passing from this world into the next by the route of death; "absent from the body, present with the Lord." Here, and then there, so infinitely more real than what has been left behind, which is now just a distant memory. For those precious minutes above the clouds it was hard to remember traffic jams on the M1 and litter and smoking power stations. That was another life, a past life. This was LIFE. This was NOW!

Over the years, I have nursed many terminally ill people and been present with them as they have drawn their last breath and felt their pulse weaken and fade away. Nothing dramatic on our side of the veil! But what must have it been like for those patients fully prepared for the next land, going through the veil? A seamless experience? Here, and then there. Here; murk, cloud, mud, pain, work. And then, there; clear, crystal, pure, joy, rest "pleasures for evermore," going on and on for ever; peace, no more pain; a Throne now seen in the midst of the rainbows and One "whose Name is Love" seated upon that Throne, waiting to welcome, One very familiar to those who have, for many a day, journeyed with Him and to Him, by faith.

Why on earth do we want to hold back our friends and family who are ill from going to such place? Or to rephrase that, why do we pray for ourselves and our sick relatives to be healed, when it means them staying on earth, and possibly further suffering at some future date, and denying them Heaven now? (Perhaps it is because we love them so much and parting is so very, very painful).

The apostle Paul said in one of his letters that he desired to depart and go to a place which he described as "far better." Let's take his word for it. After all, had he not had a glimpse already, a short flight above, a taster so to speak, of what was to come. Perhaps this happened when the crowds stoned him at Lystra and dragged him out of the city, supposing that he was dead (compare Acts 14:19 with 2 Corinthians 12:1-4). Did he taste Heaven then? Who could have tasted of Heaven and then still regard earth as home and want to remain here? Certainly not Paul, except he had unfinished work to do here given by His Lord. That was the only thing that kept him back. After all, the Lord Jesus had said, "I go to prepare a place for you," and like the wine at Cana, is not everything the Lord Jesus prepares the very best?

And then the flight was over; the plane descended through the clouds, and the voice said, "We shall be arriving at Belfast Airport at 1400 hours. The weather is overcast and the temperature is 6 degrees. Please ensure you keep your seat belts fastened until the plane is stationary. Thank you for flying with us and we wish you a safe onward journey." So it's back to earth (with just a slight bump - well done Mr. or Mrs. Pilot) and the realities of a reunion hopefully with the suitcase on the baggage carousel, the Belfast Telegraph's inevitably depressing evening headlines, and getting the car from the car park.

"Do we need bread, Sue?"

"No, only milk. We'll pull in somewhere on the way home."

Goodbye "Heaven" (for now!).

Reference: (1) Jn.19:23

31: Hallmarks of Worship

A hallmark is a stamp used by a government assay office to mark the standard of gold or silver. Purely from an individual perspective as opposed to a collective one, what are the hallmarks that indicate that our worship is true worship?

1) From the heart (see Matthew 15:8-9)
We cannot worship God acceptably from our hearts if we are not saved. Salvation through faith in our Lord Jesus Christ makes our hearts right before God, through that first and total bathing that the Lord Jesus speaks about in John 13:10, and which is described in Titus 3:5 as being "through the washing of regeneration and renewing of the Holy Spirit". But we also, as Christians, are tempted and fall into sin. Before we can worship God with "clean hands and a pure heart" (1) we must confess our sins. How thankful we are that he is "faithful and just to forgive us our sins and to cleanse us from all unrighteousness" (2). Then our hearts are ready for worship. But we have to believe God when He says "all unrighteousness"- there is no sin that is too big to be forgiven, if we have truly repented of it and confessed it to God.

But what kind of worship are we going to offer to God? It must come from our hearts and not just from our lips. There is nowhere deeper than the heart. It is the source of all that comes out of Man. No wonder the writer of Proverbs exhorts us to "keep your heart with all diligence, for out of it spring the issues of life" (3). It is the very core of our being. When we do something half-heartedly, we show that are hearts are not really in what we are doing. Half-hearted worship is no worship, for we will just be going through the motions. This was the criticism that the Lord Jesus levelled at the Pharisees - they honoured God with their lips, but that is as deep as it went. Their worship did not start in the heart - their hearts were far from God.

In worship we speak to God and for our worship to have the hallmark of true worship, deep must speak unto deep, our redeemed hearts must be bowed before God our Redeemer, and what we offer must come from the depths of our hearts.

2) "In spirit and truth" (see John 4:21-24)

God is not worshipped today at any particular geographical place ("neither on this mountain nor in Jerusalem" as Jesus told the woman at the well in John 4) or by the offering of any material sacrifices. No need then for worshippers to go on a pilgrimage bearing gifts! God, who is Spirit, is worshipped "in spirit and truth". Invisible sacrifices of praise (4) coming from the heart are offered to God through His Son, who is the "way, the truth and the life" (5). In Heaven He alone holds the office of Great High Priest and He presents our offerings of praise to God. When we worship we fill His hands "full of sweet incense beaten fine" (6). That is a supreme privilege for a redeemed saint who, as an unsaved sinner, caused those same Hands to be pierced.

As Jesus is the one and only Great High Priest appointed by God "to offer both gifts and sacrifices" (7), God will accept no other worship than that which is offered through Him, and any worship that is not offered to the God and Father of our Lord Jesus Christ, the True God, is idolatry. Paul rejoiced in the Lord when he wrote to fellow believers in Philippi, saying, "we are the circumcision, who worship God in the Spirit, rejoice in Christ Jesus, and have no confidence in the flesh" (8). True spiritual worship has divine (scriptural) truth as its hallmark.

3) "With reverence and awe" (see Hebrews 12:18-29)

Our worship is in Heaven, a needed truth to be emphasised afresh. God does not come down to be worshipped in a tent, a tin hall or in a mighty cathedral, or in any other material setting, but worshippers are taken into Heaven! Spiritual sacrifices are offered when, in Spirit, we, as true worshippers, come to Mount Zion, to the city of the Living God, the heavenly Jerusalem. That is where the Living God dwells. In a past day, that same Living God caused Mount Sinai to quake and burn with fire when He came down to speak with Moses (see also Exodus 19:18). If, godly man though he was, Moses also quaked with fear, should not we also approach God's presence with reverence and awe? He has not changed. He is holy, a consuming fire. But thankfully, He has changed us, otherwise we could not approach to worship Him.

If we have meditated on the deep meaning of the broken bread and poured-out wine and have been brought again in spirit to the cross as we remember our Lord Jesus Christ on a Lord's Day morning together, then we cannot help but be filled with reverence and awe in the light of such love.

> Such love stilling my restlessness,
> Such love, filling my emptiness,
> Such love, showing me holiness,
> O Jesus, such love.
> (Graham Kendrick)

Esther must have come trembling before King Ahasuerus until she saw that the golden sceptre was being held out, signalling her acceptance into the king's presence. We worship before a greater than King Ahasuerus and yet He in love invites us into His presence in Heaven to worship Him along with the "innumerable company of angels" and all the blessed company of Heaven. Wonderful privilege!

> 'The Holies now we enter
> In perfect peace with God.' (9)

In a day when scriptural truth can be diluted, vision lost and blessings forfeited, let us examine our worship again and test it by God's Word to see if it bears the hallmarks of true worship; from the heart, in spirit and truth, and with reverence and awe - "for the Father is seeking such to worship Him" (10).

References: (1) Ps.24:4 (2) 1 Jn.1:9 (3) Prov.4:23 (4) see Heb.13:15 (5) Jn.14:6 (6) see Lev.16:12 (7) Heb.8:3 (8) Phil.3:3 (9) Psalms, Hymns and Spiritual Songs, 94, Mrs. Peters (10) Jn.4:23

32: MALACHI – THE PROPHET WITH A WAKE-UP CALL

It was the preacher in Ecclesiastes 3 who said that there is "a time to keep silence and a time to speak" (1). Malachi was raised up by God to speak to the nation of Israel in a period of declension, and he could not keep silent but speak out the "oracle (or "burden", RV) of the word of the Lord" (2). This was to be the last word from God to His chosen nation for about 400 years until the coming of the "messenger of the covenant" (3), the Lord who would be like "a refiner's fire" and "purifier of silver" (4) to purify and refine His people so that their offerings would be pleasing to God again.

Again? So was God not finding pleasure in His people? No! Far from it! These were dark days in Israel's history; days of nominal service, cold hearts and blind eyes. Malachi prophesied to Judah after their return from Babylon, which took place in successive stages over roughly a century starting at approximately 536BC. The Northern Kingdom as an entity, who had previously been known as 'Israel', did not return from Assyrian exile; the remnant of Judah who came back from Babylon are now described as 'Israel' (5). The remnant here was the small number of faithful Jews of all tribes who responded to God's call to return from captivity.

Is the prophecy just a message for its own time? In Galatians 6:16, God's new covenant people, made up of Jews and Gentiles is described as "the Israel of God." So we listen to see if it is relevant in our own time, too, and to each one of us personally.

The format of Malachi's prophecy is a dialogue between God and His people. In response to God's words to them, they had many questions and God answers them. The Spirit of God, speaking through Malachi, was able to assess and diagnose the condition of the hearts of the people, and the questions they asked reflected the low state into which they had fallen. God's desire was to bring about repentance and revival - needed then, and now, if we are honest!

"I have loved you" was God's opening statement, and how hurtful to Him to hear the people's reply, "How have you loved us?" (6). They had been chosen by God over Esau in sovereign grace to fulfil God's purposes, and it had not been because of anything commendable in them. Nothing could frustrate God's plans. Esau's descendants who formed the nation of Edom, despite their resistance, would be judged by God for their sin against Israel and cease. (Visit the ruins of Petra in Jordan for graphic proof of God's faithfulness in keeping His word in chapter 1, verse 4.)

How reassuring to us today to know that we who, by grace, have been chosen in Christ "before the foundation of the world" (7) have a God who is a covenant-keeping God. Even if we are faithless, He remains faithful to His own character and purpose; that's the nature of our great God (8). But Israel could not see all of this; they had forgotten God's covenant promises and based their judgement on the prevailing circumstances of the time. As a small remnant, they felt their weakness. So how could God be for them? They needed their eyes to be opened!

Malachi had a hard message from God for the priests. God said that they despised His name. "How have we despised your name?" was their reply (9). It was evident in the quality of their offerings. Far from giving their best they brought the blind, lame and sick animals as sacrifices. Did they think God couldn't see? What they gave reflected the value they had put upon the person to whom they gave. No wonder God was offended.

How much time and effort do I put into my offerings of praise and worship? Are they truly 'sacrifices'? And does my weekly giving to the Lord reflect a heart that is truly grateful for all He has poured out for me? Am I giving my best? Guy Jarvie, writing in NT magazine in 1948, said about Israel in Malachi's day, "Positionally, they were at the place, but conditionally, alas, they were far away in heart" (10). This is an ever-present danger for God's people.

If the priests did not repent and reform they would be cursed; in fact, God had already cursed them, by withdrawing blessings 11). In chapter 2:4-7 God paints the picture of what He looked for in Levi, with whom He had made a covenant. A priest was to fear and reverence God, give true instruction, speak truth, walk "in peace and uprightness" (12) turn many from iniquity, guard knowledge, and seek instruction from God. God's ideals are very high but He has not lowered the bar for His priests today. That humbles me, as the Spirit of God searches my heart to reveal how far short I often fall!

In chapter 2, Malachi tells Israel that they had wearied God with their words. And when they protested, "How have we wearied him?" (v.17), his answer was that they were accusing God of delighting in evil doers and being unjust (13). They were making serious charges against God!

But not all received God's condemnation, and we read in chapter 3 that there were still some - a remnant of a remnant we might say - who "feared the Lord", who "spoke with one another" (14). God knew, and had a book of remembrance written with their names. They were His personal possession, and he would spare them "as a man spares his son who serves him" (15). It would be very clear in a future day whom the righteous and the wicked were! The day will declare it.

The book of Malachi closes with the announcement of that future day, a day of judgement for the wicked but "for you who fear my name, the sun of righteousness will rise with healing in its wings" (16). His announcement of the coming Messiah, the One who would "suddenly come to his temple" (17) should have had the effect of causing the people of God to repent, to turn their spiritual eyes upward and to look expectantly and wait (like Simeon in Luke 2) for "the consolation of Israel" and this promised "sun of righteousness" who would come to heal them of their sins by His wounds received at Calvary (18).

"How shall we return?" the people had asked God in chapter 3. This was in answer to God's loving commandment, "Return to me and I will return to you, says the LORD of Hosts" (19). Unbelieving Israel, as a nation, have still not returned and have yet to repent and receive Him whom they despised and rejected (20). That day will come! "What will their acceptance mean but life from the dead?" (21). On that day the prophesy in Malachi chapter 4:2-3 will be fully realised. What joy!

In conclusion, there is nothing 'minor' in Malachi's prophecies! His themes include God's sovereignty, God's amazing love, His inevitable judgement against sin and assessment of Israel's condition with hard, searching words for the priests, a passionate call to get right with God, and to "bring the full tithe into the storehouse" (22).

John Blanchard in his book on the minor prophets, wrote, "It is possible to read Malachi in less than ten minutes - but it is impossible to read it comfortably, as its message is as powerfully disturbing now as when it was first written" (23).

Today also we must not keep silent; it's a time to speak. God burdened His prophet Malachi with a timely message. His name translates as 'my messenger'. The apostle Paul was burdened in his day with God's message of salvation for all who would believe. His burden was "to testify to the gospel of the grace of God" (24). Are we burdened today to pass the message on?

Malachi, the last book in our Old Testament, contains a vital message from God to Israel. At the close of our New Testament scriptures we hear the apostle John's exhortation to disciples of the Lord Jesus Christ which is still vitally important today: "And now, little children, abide in him, so that when he appears we may have confidence and not shrink from him in shame at his coming. If you know that he is righteous, you may be sure that everyone who practices righteousness has been born of him" (25).

References (all Scripture references from the ESV): (1) Eccl.3:7 (2) Mal.1:1 (3) Mal.3:1 (4) Mal.3:2-3 (5) Mal.1:1 (6) Mal.1:2 (7) Eph.1:4 (8) 2 Tim.2:12-13 (9) Mal.1:6 (10) p.77 (11) Mal.2:2 (12) Mal.2:6 (13) Mal.2:17 (14) Mal.3:16 (15) Mal.3:17 (16) Mal.4:2 (17) Mal.3:1 (18) Is.53:5; 1 Pet.2:24 (19) Mal.3:7 (20) Is.53:3 (21) Rom.11:15 (22) Mal.3:10 (23) Blanchard, J., "Major Points from the Minor Prophets", E.P. Books 2012, p. 255) (24) Acts 20:24 (25) 1 Jn.2:28-29

33: APPOINTED TIMES

At the time of writing, the swifts and swallows are leaving the UK for warmer climates as winter approaches here. Instinct or the call of nature tells them that this is the time for migration.

God, in His wisdom, has appointed times for the outworking of His purposes in the world. Such a time came when "God sent forth His Son, born of a woman, born under the law" (1). It was the "fullness of time". Events unfolded in the life of our Lord Jesus according to the divine plan; God sovereignly over-ruling in the affairs of men to bring about His purposes for His Son on a daily basis. It was not only His birth that was at the appointed time and place, but every event in His life, including the place and time of His departure.

God is no less intimately involved in the lives of His People. He has a plan for Israel: "I know the plans I have for you, declares the LORD, plans for wholeness and not for evil, to give you a future and a hope" (2). He has a plan for your life and my life too.

Our disappointments are God's appointments. As Ecclesiastes 3:1-8 reminds us, in each life there are appointed times for joys and sorrows, seeking and losing, speaking and remaining silent, for action and for waiting, etc. The challenge that comes to us is to seek God's plan for our lives and to fit into it. We will only be happy when doing the will of God. We will only function properly when we find and do that for which we have been particularly and specially prepared. Experiences of life are ordained by God to achieve that, each at just the right appointed time.

Perhaps our spiritual 'instincts' are telling us that as regards this present evil world that the summer is nearly over (3). The leaves of prophecy are falling thick and fast, and we should be thinking about getting ready for the appointed time of our going - going to be with the Lord, answering the call of our Lord as He comes for His own. Maranatha!

> 'The little birds trust God, for they go singing
> From northern woods where autumn winds have blown,
> With joyous faith their trackless pathway winging
> To summer-lands of song, afar, unknown.
>
> Let us go singing, then, and not go sighing
> Since we are sure our times are in His hand,
> Why should we weep, and fear, and call it dying?
> 'Tis only flitting to a Summer-land.'
> (Anon).

References: (1) Gal.4:4 (2) Jer.29:11 ESV (3) Jer.8:20

34: FRUIT

There was a poor harvest in the apple orchards near my home this year. Some said it was the worst for 30 years, and that the frost in spring was to blame. Whatever the reason it is a cause of great sadness to an apple-grower, farmer or even a gardener when his crop fails.

He has put in so much work, selecting the right seed, plants or saplings. He has tended them through the early stages when they are so vulnerable, protecting them from attacks by insects, fungal infections, removing choking weeds and giving the right nutrients and regular irrigation. The early signs have been good; plenty of growth, thick foliage and of course the crucial blossom at the right time. And then the summer comes, and the time of expected fruits. And nothing is found! All that labour has been in vain for that year, for the whole operation was directed to one end; the production of fruit.

What can we learn from this? The Bible speaks a lot about fruit-bearing. Jesus Himself told a parable in Luke 13 about a man who had a fig tree planted in his vineyard. For three years he came looking for fruit and there was none. He gave orders for it to be cut down. But the man in charge of the vineyard begged for one more year for the fig tree. He would tend it and feed it and then, if it still bore no fruit, he would cut it down. No doubt he still had hopes for the tree on which he had spent so much time and care. Something of the purposes and the character of God come out in the telling of this parable. Firstly, the Lord's ultimate objective in saving us through the death of His Son is that we should bear fruit, and secondly, the Lord's great patience with us.

It is very disappointing to experience a crop failure. I experienced it this year myself with my blackcurrant bushes. It is also three years since I planted them and again this year I have looked for the lovely vitamin C-rich berries from which to make pies and jam and drinks, and there are none. (I think I may have pruned them at the wrong time: our heavenly Father never makes any mistakes!)

Alongside them other bushes, whitecurrants and gooseberries, have produced an abundant harvest, and it has been a race to see who gets them first, the blackbirds and thrushes or us! (Actually there's enough for both!). There is a special joy in filling up a big bowl of freshly picked summer fruits and carrying them into the kitchen. It must be the same kind of satisfaction that the apple-grower experiences when he sees his large wooden crates filled to the top with apples being transported away for packing or crushing for juice; or the satisfaction the farmer gets as he sees the trailers full of newly harvested grain leaving the field for the silo.

Harvest thanksgiving has its truth in a very real experience in the heart of the one who expended such labour into the production of the crop, and who also sought the blessing of the One who has the power to give or to withhold the sun and the rain at the right time, and who gives strength for the daily labour. But I'm sure nothing exceeds the joy of the Lord of the harvest, for which He expended His very best, His Son, His all, when the sheaves are brought safely into His store - the harvest of souls! Was it for this joy that the Bible tells us Jesus endured the cross and despised its shame? He was able to see ahead to the harvest, when, in resurrection glory, he would see the results of the "labour of His soul, and be satisfied" (1). His rejection and affliction at the hands of men, and His forsaking by His Father on the cross would all be worthwhile.

That is a joy all the redeemed can in some measure enter into, when we make it our goal to be soul-winners. We can have the joy of leading someone, young or old, to the Lord for salvation. We can be like Joseph who was described by his father Jacob as a fruitful bough by a well, hanging over a wall (2), and bring pleasure to God who saved, tended, protected, fed and filled us with His Spirit for this very purpose, and with great patience waits for us to bring forth fruit to His glory. "By this My Father is glorified, that you bear much fruit; so you will be my disciples" (3).

References: (1) Is.53:11 (2) Gen.49:22 (3) Jn.15:8

35: FOR TIMES OF BEREAVEMENT

"And when he rose from prayer, he came to the disciples and found them sleeping for sorrow." (1)

Various stages in the bereavement process have been well documented. At different times there may be feelings of numbness and unbelief that it is really happening. Anger, sometimes towards God for allowing a loss to occur might be mixed with bitterness. Or the "If you stop this happening, I promise I will…," scenario which reflects a desperate bargaining attempt to try to prevent the loss from happening.

There is a huge emotional and physical cost when suffering grief, especially when the one who has gone was greatly loved. It takes its toll, as those readers who have suffered a bereavement of some kind will know all too well. As well as losing a loved one through death, bereavement can be through a loss of a job, of marriage partner through separation or divorce, a realisation that a hoped for ideal relationship has not been achieved, loss of home through inability to meet mortgage repayments, loss of children through emigration, and loss of direction in life when goals and ambitions are not realised. These are also all potential experiences of bereavement with the accompanying emotional and physical effects. Increased tiredness and more sleep than is normal may well be one natural way of responding to loss.

The disciples were going through a hard, sad experience. They had many valid reasons to be sorrowful, just as you, dear reader, may be nursing a sorrowful, breaking heart at this present time. Jesus, their beloved Master and Lord was sorrowful. Calvary was drawing near. Taking Peter and James and John aside, he said to them in Gethsemane, "My soul is very sorrowful, even unto death; remain here and watch with me" (2). They saw his distress and this would make them distressed. It is the response of a loving heart to "weep with those who weep" (3). Then whilst their Lord and Master agonised in prayer in Gethsemane, deeply sorrowing and no doubt physically weary, they fell asleep.

In his dissertations with them in the upper room, they had heard that one of them would betray him. Peter specifically had heard that he was going to deny three times that he even knew His Lord! In the upper room, during the Passover meal, Jesus had newly instituted the 'remembrance' or 'breaking of the bread' which they would keep after his resurrection and the giving of the Spirit at Pentecost, to remember him in the broken bread and poured-out wine. This, no doubt, had graphically impressed upon their struggling minds and hearts the sad reality of his soon to be accomplished suffering and death. They were not yet mature enough in their understanding to accept this as being in the will of God, or to realise the significance of it for themselves as the basis for God's salvation.

In the bereavement experience when a loved one is dying or has died, there is a journey taking place both for the one facing death and for those who are left. Those privileged enough to be close to someone who is diagnosed with a terminal illness have the opportunity to walk a little of that journey with them. For the person who is dying and for those left to mourn, the ultimate goal of the journey is to reach acceptance; for, as the poet Amy Carmichael has penned in one of her poems, "In acceptance lieth peace" (4).

Openness, honesty and a willingness to face the issues raised by the impending separation are a help to all involved in completing this journey into peace. Sensitivity, too, is needed to meet the needs of children who also need to grieve. It is also possible, albeit for right motives of love and concern, to be over-protective when someone close is dying. Children old enough to understand need to be sensitively included. They, too, have a journey to complete.

In the west at least, death has generally become a taboo subject, whereas it is part of the reality of living to be faced, not swept under the carpet. For some, 'healing' of the emotions may take a long time. Those who say, usually sincerely, 'Time is a great healer" may be underestimating the deep and lasting effects that a bereavement may have on those left behind with an empty armchair. <u>Time</u> and the Lord are far more likely to bring the traveller to the desired haven of acceptance and peace.

Enabling a bereaved person to talk through their experiences may be the best help that can be offered by a caring friend, as well as praying for them. To be a good and patient listener is a precious gift. Appropriate verses of Scripture, read or given at the right time, are a source of comfort. "Weeping may tarry for the night, but joy comes with the morning" (5). The disciples sorrow at the death of Jesus would soon be swallowed up in the joy of glad realisation of the resurrection morning. And the work of God's Spirit in their hearts would produce the fruit of love, joy and peace.

In the rich tapestry of life that our God is weaving in each redeemed life, the dark threads are as needful as the threads of gold and silver in the pattern that God has planned for each of our lives. Could it be that to get to know Jesus better, the One described as "a man of sorrows" (6), we too have to experience sorrow in some measure in our own lives, though our sufferings can never be compared with those experienced by the Lord Jesus Christ. Yes, we will not get all the answers down here to our 'whys' but faith takes us forward to a future day when all will be explained. Then "sleeping for sorrow" will be fully exchanged for: "when I awake I shall be satisfied with your likeness" (7). And, "In your presence there is fullness of joy" (8).

Travelling by train through the mountains and valleys of the English Lake District to attend the funeral of an elderly Christian lady in Windermere, a number of years ago, I had the experience of seeing the sun suddenly break through the clouds of an otherwise overcast day and flood the valley with glorious sunshine. That graphically reminded me that my friend had gone home to glory, which is far better. There is still sunshine in the valley of grief for those who trust in the Lord. David, the shepherd king, no doubt speaking from personal experience, could write those well-known words from Psalm 23 which have been a source of comfort to so many: "Yea, thou I walk through the valley of the shadow of death, I will fear no evil: for thou art with me and thy rod and thy staff they comfort me" (9).

References: (all references from the ESV, unless otherwise stated): (1) Lk.22:45 (2) Matt.26:38 (3) Rom.12:15 (4) From "Towards Jerusalem", the poems of Amy Carmichael (5) Ps.30:5 (6) Is.53:3 (7) Ps.17:15 (8) Ps.16:11 (9) Ps.23:4 KJV

36: THE SECRETS OF THE HEART

Technological advances in medical equipment have resulted in being able to scan in great detail most parts of the human body so that physical problems can be diagnosed and then treated. But no-one looks into the heart and examines its secrets! That is, no-one except God!

When Samuel was sent by God to choose one of the eight sons of Jesse to be the anointed king over Israel, Samuel's natural inclination was to judge the best candidate from outward appearances, which in this case, in Samuel's opinion, was Eliab. "But the Lord said to Samuel, "Do not look on his appearance or on the height of his stature, because I have rejected him. For the Lord sees not as man sees: man looks on the outward appearance, but the Lord looks on the heart" (1).

Sadly, we too so often judge one another by external factors. How wonderful that the Lord can look into the heart of a man or woman and see what is there, but also how sobering too! Every heart contains secrets that we would prefer God not to know! But the writer of the Psalm says God "knows the secrets of the heart" (2).

The Lord Jesus Christ, as God the Son with all the attributes of divinity, including omniscience, could look into the hearts of the people that he met or observed and read their motives. One day whilst sitting opposite the offering box in the temple of God in Jerusalem (3), he observed a poor widow woman putting in two small copper coins to be used in God's service. She must have loved God with all her heart for Jesus knew that she had put into the collection all that she had, leaving nothing to live on! (How does my giving compare to that?) Others might compare her gift with the big amounts that the wealthy were giving, and ridicule her contribution. But not Jesus! What love he saw in that poor woman's heart, and what faith! In His eyes, others had only given 'dog-ends' (cigarette butts) in comparison to her giving.

On another occasion, in Lazarus's house in Bethany (4), Mary, Lazarus's sister, sat at the Lord's feet and listened to His teaching, making the most of having the Lord in her home. She had a thirsty heart, and wanted to drink in the living word of God coming from the mouth of the Word incarnate. She had weighed up in her heart what was the best way to occupy her time. The choice was between chores and communion with her Lord. Mary had chosen the "good portion." The Lord knew that her motive was not to avoid doing housework or to over burden Martha, but to learn of him, and He said that it would not be taken away from her. The Lord has always had His "lovers" like Mary, whose hearts are drawn to Him, who have chosen the "good portion" and He deeply appreciates and rewards their devotion.

Think of the most treasured item you own, perhaps a treasured heirloom. Would you, like the woman who came to the Lord with her alabaster jar containing precious ointment (5), be prepared to give it up to show your love for the Lord? Perhaps it was the only precious thing she owned, a surety for her future welfare maybe? What made her so determined to break her jar and anoint the head of the Lord Jesus Christ as He reclined at the table? Was it love for Him? Whilst her actions only attracted criticism from the mercenary-minded, the Lord, who knew the secrets of her heart and what motivated her to do such a lovely thing, anointing his body for burial and filling the house with perfume, commended her: "she has done a beautiful thing to me" (6).

Have I ever made any real sacrifices for the Lord, out of the love of my heart? A challenging thought! If not, perhaps my heart is too small and too mean. Long before Christiaan Barnard (the first surgeon to perform a heart transplant operation in 1967) was on the scene, God was able to give a change of heart to those who came to Him in repentance and faith; yes, a new heart! Some, Pharisees and scribes, who came to the Lord Jesus, He described as 'hypocrites'. He quoted to them the prophecy of Isaiah: "This people honours me with their lips, but their heart is far from me; in vain do they worship me, teaching as doctrines the commandments of men" (7).

Whatever the particular nature of our sin, only a spiritual birth from above can provide us with the new heart we so badly need, in exchange for the one that is so far from Him. It would be tragic in our own day to go through the motions of worshipping God but for our own hearts to be far from Him. Some of us, brought up as 'nominal Christians' in a 'Christian' country, have experienced that condition, from which we have been delivered by the grace of God.

Jesus also knows when there is a wrestling match going on inside the heart. One day a man came to Jesus seeking an answer to the question of how to receive eternal life (8). Jesus knew he was a genuine seeker, but also that he was very rich. Mark records that Jesus, "looking at him, loved him". He wanted to set him free, for Jesus, knowing his heart, knew that he was a prisoner to his riches. The love of money is an ever-present danger, for disciples now and then, a subtle trap. So Jesus instructed him to sell everything he owned, give to the poor and come and become Jesus' follower. His riches proved to be too strong for him. He went away sorrowful and that day Satan won the wrestling match and kept his prisoner. We will meet many crossroads in life where the Devil will bargain with us to turn us from the right path.

Sometimes, even as Christians, we struggle, suffer failure, give in to temptation, take the wrong path and experience sorrow because of our sins. We long for restoration, renewal and revival in our hearts. We feel like a "bruised reed" or a "smoking flax" (9), of no use to God. That's what Peter must have felt like as he lived with the consequences of his denial of the Lord on the night of Jesus' betrayal and arrest. But the Lord knew the secrets of Peter's heart, knew he had a broken heart, knew he was repentant and, on the beach in Galilee, assured him that he was both forgiven and restored to service (10).

The words of the Lord, spoken again through Isaiah, could well have applied to Peter: "I dwell in the high and holy place, and also with him who is of a contrite and lowly spirit, to revive the spirit of the lowly, and to revive the heart of the contrite" (11). If you feel that in some measure you, too, have let your Lord down, take God's words and apply them to yourself. In the Lord Jesus, God has revealed to us that He has a merciful heart. We thank God for that and for Jesus our Lord whose heart was broken on the cross (see Psalm 69:20) for our sakes.

A prayer:
> Search me, O God, and know my heart today;
> Try me, O Saviour, know my thoughts, I pray;
> See if there be some wicked way in me:
> Cleanse me from every sin, and set me free. (12)
> (E.J. Orr)

References (all Scripture references from the ESV): (1) 1 Sam.16:7 (2) Ps.44:21 (3) Mk.12:41-44 (4) Lk.10:38-42 (5) Mk.14:3-9 (6) v.6 (7) Matt.15:8-9 (8) Mk.10:17-22 (9) Matt.12:20 (10) Jn.21:15-19 (11) Is.57:15b (12) From the hymn "Search Me, O God"

37: DO YOU LOVE ME? (PART ONE)

The storyline is set in Czarist Russia in the early years of the last century. Anatevka is a small village in a farming community. Amongst its population is a close-knit group of orthodox Jews, steeped in the traditions that have held them together for centuries. Tevye and Golde are looking to the village "Match-maker" to find husbands for their daughters, following traditional practice (today a dating agency might aim to fulfil a similar role). For this was how Tevye, a simple farmer and milkman, and his wife, Golde were brought together, by a Matchmaker in the village, meeting for the first time on their wedding day! However, against all accepted traditions, three of their daughters choose their own husbands, having fallen in love. Tevye and Golde are shocked! They have never heard of such a thing, going against all tradition. Marrying for love? "Unheard of!"

In the stage musical "Fiddler on the Roof", from which this scene is extracted, as a result of what their daughters have done, Tevye, reflecting on what has happened to his daughters, poses the question to Golde, "Do you love me?" They have been married for twenty-five years, and never once have they told each other that they love each other! Golde, in the words of the song they then sing together, recalls that she has washed his clothes, cleansed his house, borne his children, fought with him, and starved with him! But never has this question been asked before; "Do you love me?" The duet ends with Golde saying, "I suppose I do!" And as Tevye acknowledges that he, too, must love Golde, for he has lived with her and provided for her for twenty-five years, through good times and bad, the realisation that they do love each other, though it was never said, fills them with joy!

Saying it doesn't change anything, but just knowing that they love and care for each other is enough. Their love had grown and lasted over the years, and the ingredients of that recipe are basically the same for all successful marriages, however they start!

This chapter, and the two following, outlines what those ingredients are in the hope that someone's marriage will be strengthened as a result of considering them.

Love and Affection
Love is a very hard thing to define. It is made up of the emotional and the physical. It shows itself in different love 'languages'. Someone may express love through what they do, rather than through what they say. Kind, thoughtful acts may be the way a person says 'I love you'. It may be a bunch of flowers or a welcoming home with well-cooked meals. Like Tevye and Golde in "Fiddler on the Roof," who were brought together in an arranged marriage, as tradition dictated in the culture of that time and place, love may have grown up over many years, showing itself in unselfish caring for the spouse and family, making sacrifices when necessary for the well-being of the other.

Whatever way it is expressed, the emotional feelings that may have characterised the beginning of a relationship will change as time goes by. So called 'puppy love' (or *'eros'*, the Greek word for 'romantic love') will need to grow, mature and deepen if it is to stand the tests that time brings.

And that is why love and affection go hand in hand. Affection is crucial in a marriage relationship. Tender feelings toward the other need to be expressed in numerous small ways; the occasional held hands when out walking, the warm embrace, the spontaneous kiss, for example. These are important throughout married life, not just when a couple are young or newly married. Marriage is not a business arrangement whereby two people live together and run an efficient home. It is a relationship. Affection for one another must always be at the centre. It is the food that the tender plant feeds on and grows and strengthens.

When affection goes out of a relationship, trouble lies ahead. Love making, if it happens at all, will just be 'mechanical' for the true love and affection that undergird it are missing. Although basic physical needs are being met, the sexual appetite temporarily satisfied, the deeper emotional needs are not. When one or other of the partners is not having these needs fulfilled, he or she may then unconsciously or consciously begin to look elsewhere. The heart may then be drawn to another, a friend, a close colleague, and then marital unfaithfulness becomes a real danger. Some marriages may survive in this atmosphere but then are really marriages in name only, because love and affection are missing from the core. Two people are living under the same roof, but that is all.

Commitment

Every marriage starts with a spoken statement of commitment: e.g. "I take you, to be my wife, (my husband) to have and to hold, from this day forward, for better, for worse, for richer, for poorer, in sickness and in health, to love and to cherish, till death us do part, according to God's holy law. In the presence of God I make this vow."

In that form of words from a traditional church marriage service, vows of commitment are taken by both partners. But those are only words! Words have to be translated into actions. That commitment has to be shown as real through all the changing circumstances of married life. Many have found it to be costly, especially when one partner becomes ill, needs long-term care, or when the dreamed-of married life didn't work out as expected. Commitment means staying the course, even when times are tough. When vows are taken before God, then that is a serious matter. In society today many drop their partners as soon as they get tired of them, much as they would think about changing the wallpaper for a fresh design, or the car for a new model! As men get older, and their wives are not as attractive to them physically as they once were, the temptation to look around for someone younger becomes a danger. Woman may be drawn to someone they feel understands them better and is more caring.

The Book of Ruth describes Ruth's commitment towards Naomi, her mother-in-law, when Naomi decides to return from Moab, Ruth's home country, to Naomi's ancestral home in Bethlehem. Ruth loves Naomi, and hard times have come upon them both through bereavements. Ruth expresses her commitment in the well-known words found in chapter 1:16-17:

"Do not urge me to leave you or to return from following you. For where you go, I will go, and where you lodge, I will lodge. Your people shall be my people, and your God, my God. Where you die, I will die, and there will I be buried. May the Lord do so to me and more also if anything but death parts me from you."

God honoured Ruth's commitment, as the end of their story in the Bible makes clear.

38: DO YOU LOVE ME? (PART TWO)

One outstanding feature of marriage is that it should result in joy. To be joyful is a fruit of the Spirit of God at work, so therefore that fruit should be evident in a marriage relationship. If a couple are miserable together, it is a sure sign that all is not well between them. Christians can sometimes put on a "brave face" to the world, and even to other Christians; but left to themselves, and on their own, there is constant bickering and falling out. This does nothing to glorify God or advertise marriage as being God-ordained and given for the mutual benefit of both the man and the woman.

Faithfulness

Trust is an essential ingredient in a happy marriage. In one popular TV show screened in the UK, couples are brought onto the set and their personal relationship problems are exposed and explored, often amidst angry words and tears. It is often a sad exposure of a failed and broken relationship, with many being hurt as a consequence. Frequently one partner demands that the other take a lie-detector test. They have lost their trust in the other. They suspect unfaithfulness. Suspicion is slowly poisoning their relationship. Once trust has gone, the relationship is heading for the rocks! If I cannot trust my partner, I will always be on the watch for evidence of unfaithfulness. This becomes worse if lies are being told to cover behaviour that one partner is hiding. We know who the Bible describes as "the father of lies" (1)! So behind the scenes, but very active, the Devil is attacking and destroying that which is of God, wrecking relationships, spreading unhappiness and bringing dishonour to God's name in the process.

Marriage breakdown is commonplace in western society today, and Christians are not immune in this area. So it is essential for each partner to be trustworthy. No inappropriate relationships must be formed that would undermine the marital relationship. Can I truly say that I have not behaved with someone else in a way that should be reserved for my partner only, the one to whom I am committed by marriage? If one partner suspects that inordinate affection is being given to another, then cracks will open up, jealousy will arise, and the foundations of the marriage will begin to give way. So-called 'flirting' may seem harmless enough, but it may be sowing the seeds of suspicion and distrust that will grow into a major issue in a future day.

But what if one partner does fail and develop a secret relationship? Unfaithful behaviour found out is a severe test for any marriage, and even for Christians - some are unable to forgive. That is a sad ending! Many, especially children, will be involved in the hurt that ensues. For the guilty partner, there is, if sought, forgiveness with God. The blood of God's Son cleanses from all sin according to God's promise (2), upon true repentance and confession. David, the king of Israel, sinned grievously, repented, and sought forgiveness and cleansing (3). This was granted, but there were consequences in his life, and unfaithfulness may leave lasting damage.

For the one sinned against, God's special grace is available, and is needed, for the hurt and disappointment will go very deep. But with God's help, and with time, a relationship can be restored if both parties are willing to begin again. Sometimes both partners share a measure of responsibility for the breakdown of a relationship, and lessons need to be learned by both.

So be careful young man, young woman, older man, and older woman. Your marriage is precious, fragile, and easily damaged. If it was something you were sending through the post you would label the package: FRAGILE. HANDLE WITH CARE!

References (all Scripture references from the ESV): (1) Jn.8:44 (2) 1 Jn.1:9 (3) Ps.51; 2 Sam.12:13-14

39: DO YOU LOVE ME? (PART THREE)

Your marriage is worth so much that God has used it as the chief example in Scripture to describe the relationship of Christ, the Bridegroom, with His Church, the bride (1). No wonder the Devil targets Christian marriages!

If you are going through genuine difficulties and realise you need help, then you both should be humble enough to seek that help rather than running away from the situation. Professional marriage counselling may be in order to fully explore why difficulties have arisen. Christian counsellors will have skills that enable both of you to solve your problems in confidence and hopefully move on.

Sometimes a marriage can be stronger for having being 'healed' just as a broken leg can be stronger when the bones have been reset and healed together. So don't lose hope if some of what is written here applies to you and to your situation. But there has to be an acceptance that a problem exists and a willingness to seek help together.

Marriage is a state in which two persons become 'one'. In the Book of Genesis, after God had created the man, He made, from the rib of the man, a woman, "and brought her to the man. The man said, "this at last is bone of my bones and flesh of my flesh;

she shall be called Woman, because she was taken out of Man. Therefore a man shall leave his father and his mother, and hold fast to his wife, and they shall become one flesh" (2). This union as ordained here by God as the state in which two married people live together, is much more than a physical union. Physical, emotional and spiritual bonds are involved in the union of two into one.

A successful marriage contains essential ingredients and if only one is left out, it will not be as God intended. This chapter is written for Christians, disciples of the Lord Jesus who, even in their unmarried state, should have their personal relationship with God sustained and blessed through quiet times of reading God's Word and prayer. In coming together in marriage, these habits should continue but also include times of praying and reading together. This will encourage shared spiritual goals and be mutually beneficial. Each has something to enrichen the marriage bond. Husbands are to love their wives, "as Christ loved the church and have Himself up for her" (3). They are to "love their wives as their own bodies" (4). Wives are to "submit" or to be in subjection to their husbands, "as to the Lord" (5). There is no thought of inferiority here (the Lord Jesus was in subjection to His Father but was equal with God in the Godhead). Subjection recognises the Lordship of Christ in the marriage bond, and that brings God's blessing to both partners in the marriage, for it glorifies Him.

The Apostle Peter, in his instructions to Christian husbands, describes their wives as "heirs with you of the grace of life" (6). So cherish those ingredients of tender love and affection, the long-term commitment, the true and faithful heart, openness and honesty with each other, selflessly putting the interests of the other first, and serving God together.

And finally, as Teyve and Golde discovered, may joy be the garland that adorns the lives of all of us whom God has blessed with a marriage partner! In such a marriage it will not be necessary for the question to be asked: "Do you love me?" The answer will be obvious! But it's good just to say it sometimes too!

Probably every married couple have their ups and downs. My wife and I certainly have and the lessons shared in these chapters are the result of learning these things ourselves. We acknowledge how patient God has been and still is with us, and that He is still at work in our lives. Day by day we experience God's grace as He moulds us into the people He wants us to be, much as the potter forms the clay on the wheel into the vessel he has planned to make.

References (all Scripture references from the ESV: (1) Eph.5:22-32; Rev.19:7-8 (2) Gen.2:23 (3) Eph.5:25 (4) Eph.5:28 (5) Eph.5:22 (6) 1 Pet.3:7

POSTSCRIPT: It may be that, having read these chapters, you have become aware that God has been left out of your marriage and that you are not certain that you have a personal relationship with God. To become a Christian, there has to be an acknowledgement of personal sin in your life. This is what causes a barrier between us and God, and it was to do put this right that God sent His Son into the world. The Bible, God's Word, tells us that sin has been the major problem for every living person since the first "married" couple, Adam and Eve, disobeyed God's clear commandment. Sin always brings serious consequences. It did for Adam and Eve and will in our own lives too if not forgiven.

Jesus came to be the Saviour by bearing the penalty that sin deserves. On the cross Jesus finished the work that God had given Him to do: "For Christ also suffered once for sins, the righteous for the unrighteous, that he might bring us to God..." (1 Pet.3:18). God looks for a personal response from us to what He has done. By being repentant of our sins, and receiving Jesus by faith as a personal act, God is able and willing to give us a new start in life. Not only is our guilt dealt with but God's Holy Spirit, who has been working in our hearts to convict us of our sins, now comes to live within us. This is a radical change! The promise that we read in the Bible says: "Therefore, if anyone is in Christ, he is a new creation. The old has passed away; behold the new has come" (2 Cor.5:17).

Now, with a new life to live, and with God's Spirit in our hearts, and with God's Word as our guide, we can begin to discover how to live this new life that God has purchased for us, at so much cost to Himself. If you have responded to this message of God's love, and know that you are 'born again' or 'saved' but that your partner is not a believer, then begin today to pray for him or her, because it will make a big difference if you are building your married lives on the same foundation - that is, faith in the Lord Jesus Christ. You can begin to pray together, read God's Word together, meet with other Christians together, and share the same hopes and ideals together! Then you will begin to experience what it really means to become 'one'!

40: LOSING HEART

Losing heart is about becoming discouraged. Have you ever started on some project, assignment or new venture, or even a new year's resolution, and then, at some point you have lost heart and given up? When our hearts are not in something, it soon becomes dull, routine, a chore, and eventually we may lose the motivation to continue completely. Even half-heartedness achieves nothing! On a mundane level, it may be something as simple as losing heart to keep up a healthy living routine that was designed to restore physical fitness. After the initial enthusiasm waned, for whatever reason, we lose heart. Perhaps the bathroom weighing scales never seem to register a change!

When it comes to following the Lord and spiritual things, it is a crucially important matter, for it affects our present service and future rewards. There is a lot to cause Christians to lose heart today (just as there was in Paul's day); small churches, little fruit to faithful sowing, personal failure, increased anti-Christian attitudes all around us, and the increased physical weakness that comes with illness and old age.

The wonderful light and life God has blessed us with is truly "in jars of clay" as Paul, in 2 Corinthians 4:7, describes these bodies in which God's Spirit resides; i.e. fragile, breakable, prone to sin, very earthy in substance, like earthenware pottery vessels!

However, Paul puts all these things into perspective by putting them on the weighing scales. On the other side is the eternal weight of glory that lies ahead of us (1)! Which do you think outweighs the other? "So", Paul concludes, "we do not lose heart. Even though our outward nature is wasting away, our inner nature is being renewed day by day" (2).

By fixing our eyes on Jesus (I sometimes find it helpful to look up when I pray, for Jesus is at the right hand of God on the throne of Heaven!) and by laying up treasure in Heaven, our hearts will be in the right place. Consequently, though we may experience setbacks from time to time in our practical service, we will be encouraged not to lose heart in living out the Christian life down here, with all its complexities and challenges, to the glory of God. One day it will all be worthwhile.

References (all Scripture references from the ESV): (1) 2 Cor.4:17 (2) v.16

41: THE BREATH OF GOD

The fire was burning very low in the fire-place. The cause was too much wood and coal choking the flame. The remedy was to create a current of air. As a result, a few minutes later the dying fire was transformed into a lively blaze, warming the room and giving light and comfort on a cold winter's day.

All that was needed was a current of air to fan the fire, and as I considered this fact, I thought about the desire of many to see revival among the people of God today. We all long to be living Spirit-filled, fruitful Christian lives. We long that the churches we are part of might be having an impact on the areas in which we live, worship and witness. We live in the midst of a world that is on the one hand abounding in temptations for the Christian trying to live a holy life, and on the other hand filled with people crying out for a meaning and purpose to life. Are our churches lively and warm, attracting the lost to turn to the Lord Jesus Christ as the answer to their deepest needs? If not, it's a condition we need to be deeply concerned about.

Surely it must start with you and me. We need the Holy Spirit's fullness to revive our spiritual lives. It was the breath of God that breathed life into Adam: God breathed into his nostrils the breath of life (1). The Lord Jesus breathed on His disciples on the evening of the first day of the week when He appeared to them after His resurrection saying, "Peace to you! As the Father has sent Me, I also send you." And when He had said this, He breathed on them, and said to them, "Receive the Holy Spirit" (2). They were to be His sent ones to a lost and dying world. They needed the power of the Holy Spirit who was to come to indwell, fill and anoint them on the day of Pentecost, seven weeks later. An old hymn says:

> Breathe on me, Breath of God,
> Fill me with life anew,
> That I may love what Thou dost love,
> And do what Thou wouldst do. (3)

The Lord Jesus loved the multitudes of people who came to Him, and had compassion on them. His heart went out to them. His love burned like a bright fire, it was unquenchable. We need that same love to be shed abroad in our hearts by the Holy Spirit to motivate us to follow the example of the Lord Jesus, and not to give up. The hymn continues:

> Breathe on me, Breath of God,
> Until my heart is pure,
> Until with thee I will one will,
> To do and to endure.

> Breathe on me, Breath of God.
> Till I am wholly Thine,
> Until this earthly part of me
> Glows with Thy fire divine. (3)

How are we to experience this in our lives and in our

churches? Surely it must be by repentance for sin, waiting on God in prayer, immersing ourselves deeply in His Word, opening our hearts to the searching of the Spirit, and willingness to make ourselves available to God as living sacrifices (4). What is the alternative? Smouldering, clogged lives; dull, lifeless churches. It is unthinkable! We were not called for this. Amy Carmichael in her poem expressed desire that should find an echo in our own hearts:

> Give me the love that leads the way,
> The faith that nothing can dismay,
> The hope no disappointments tire,
> The passion that will burn like fire,
> Let me not sink to be a clod;
> Make me Thy fuel, Flame of God. (5)

References: (1) Gen.2:7 (2) Jn.20:21-22 (3) Edwin Hatch (4) Rom.12:1 (5) From Towards Jerusalem by Amy Carmichael, S.P.C.K.

42: CARES

We all have cares in life. Some seem to be burdened with more cares than others. Cares can be made up of struggling with an illness, mental or physical, or having to look after someone else who is dependent, through old age, handicap or infirmity. Others have employment and financial worries. Cares can develop into deep anxieties and fears and have a depressing effect. Are you burdened with a care of responsibility? Even the Apostle Paul found the care of all the churches a continual source of anxiety to him (1). You may have cares that no-one is aware of, that you carry alone.

The Apostle Peter wrote in one of his letters, "Casting all your care upon him, because he careth for you" (2). Neither Peter, nor Paul or any of the other Apostles had a care-free life. Indeed, God had not promised it. Job was a righteous man who had many troubles in his life too. He wrote "But man is born unto trouble, as the sparks fly upward. But as for me, I would seek unto God, and unto God would I commit my cause" (3).

At the time of the year when I am writing this, the autumn leaves are falling thick and fast. Every day sees the garden paths covered. The only way to cope with them is to sweep them away before they accumulate too thickly. It's a daily job at this time of the year. And what about our accumulating cares? These, too, need to be dealt with on a regular basis. Our loving heavenly Father already knows our trying circumstances, but we need to unload our cares to Him to stop them overwhelming us. How do we "cast all our cares upon Him"? Well surely it must be in our daily quiet time with the Lord when we share with Him all the things that are on our minds and hearts.

He understands. Sometimes He can be the only one who does, as no other man or woman, brother or sister, can exactly stand in our shoes and know perfectly our inner feelings. He sympathises, but more than that, he is "touched" with the feeling of our "infirmities" (4) and He is able to touch us back, not necessarily to take away our cares and instantly solve our problems, but to put them into perspective for us and give us the grace to cope. And notice, it's ALL our cares that we have to cast upon Him. There is nothing too small. What one may experience as just another mole-hill is often to another a very real mountain. And there is nothing too big either.

A few years ago I was asked to make a plaque out of pottery for a young wife and mother to place on her wall at home. In that household were young children and the father was suffering from incurable cancer. The young woman asked me to write on the wall plaque the words "In His time, all things are possible". I have never forgotten those words. They illuminate a wonderful spiritual truth don't they, that there is nothing impossible with God. Jesus Himself said so, when speaking to His disciples (5) and that He is working out His own purposes in our lives for our eternal blessing. But it's in His time. God's timetable is not always the one we would prefer.

Cares are very weighty things to have to carry. How marvellous then to be able to view them with an eternal perspective. Paul, reviewing his own and others sufferings and cares in this present world could write, "For our light affliction, which is for the moment, worketh for us more and more exceedingly an eternal weight of glory; while we look not at the things which are seen but at the things which are not seen; for the things that are seen are temporal; but the things that are not seen are eternal" (6).

If for you and me the scales seem to be heavily loaded with cares, then with what joyful anticipation we can look ahead to the day when the Judge of all the earth will do right (7) and an eternal weight of glory will far outweigh the present weight of cares.

References: (1) 2 Cor.11:28 (2) 1 Pet.5:7 KJV (3) Job 5:7 RV (4) Heb.4:15 RV (5) Matt.19:26 (6) 2 Cor.4:17-18 RV (7) Gen.18:25

43: GHOSTS

Ghosts! I come across them all the time! Every time I take a walk to a local beauty spot I see them. And here are some just over the hill from here, in an old derelict cottage hidden in the trees. What am I talking about? Well, at the local beauty spot, alongside the river, an old canal used to run, now partially filled in but identifiable here and there by disused stone locks hidden in the undergrowth, and an occasional lock-keeper's cottage now upgraded and modernised to be a "desirable country cottage with many interesting features".

And when I take a walk along that way, I imagine the scene as it used to be in the 1800's when it was a fully working canal. I see the canal busy with barges, pulled by horses along the tow path, loaded with goods for the linen mills of old Ireland, and carrying coal from the coal-fields. I see and hear the simple country people of that time, going about their daily business and the countryside, now quiet and overgrown, but then busy with industry of one kind or another and the canal at the centre of a thriving community. All that has gone; transport has switched to the motorways; only the 'ghosts' (the memories) remain! So for 'ghosts' read 'memories' of people in the past!

And the tiny tumbledown cottage over the hill? Well that was home to a family of four children and their parents. The parents have gone home to heaven to better mansions, but the children are still around, grown men and woman living in modern houses, some with families of their own and going to the little church that meets nearby in a hall in a field. I sit with them each week to remember the Lord Jesus Christ at "the Breaking of the Bread." My wife and I sometimes pass that cottage; it's used now by one of the sons as a store for his green-grocery business. It's hard to imagine how a big family could have been brought up in that little "two-bedroom-outside-loos-no-electric-and-carry-the-water-from-the-well" dwelling. But they were.

And I see and hear their happy 'ghosts' every time I pass that way and stick my head in the ruined doorway. I smell the peat on the fire, the wheaten bread in the oven, and hear the singing of hymns as the mother busied herself with her daily chores. No telly in those days! Just long hard work broken by simple country pleasures, passing neighbours to chat to, and the joy of meeting with other believers for the regular gatherings for prayer and praise and hearing the Word of God. The scripture text on the living room and bed-room walls, were reminders that the Lord and His Word were at the centre of their lives and expectations.

The Irish countryside is dotted with these derelict cottages, disused mills and the canals that linked them together and everywhere the 'ghosts' that once peopled them, a part of the history of a people and its development. Is there anything to learn from these reflections of an age that has passed? Yes, I think there is. In the life of a believer in the Lord Jesus Christ too, according to the Word of God, some things have passed away. "If any man is in Christ he is a new creation, the old has passed away; behold, the new has come" (1).

Do you ever, like me, look back, perhaps many years, to the person you used to be and think, "Well, that seems to me to be a person living in a different age"? It is true that, as believers, God will not hold our sinful past against us in a future day. It was dealt with at the cross of Christ, and thankfully those old things that were the outcome of the sinful nature have passed away. But we are what we are, and part of what we are now is because of what we once were and the life we have lived, with its changing scenes and experiences. History makes the present very rich for those who want to tap into its rich vein.

Just as the present countryside is a heritage from an industrial or agricultural past, peopled by 'ghosts' from another age, so your life and my life has its memories too, experiences we have had, and people we have met and been friendly with that have led us to be the people we are today - unique individual human beings, with individual and unique experiences of life with its joys and sorrows.

There is only one you and only one me. You and I are unique, 'a new creation' if we are saved through faith, and will surely carry that uniqueness on, as we are transformed by God's Spirit into the image of the Son of God, who loved us and gave himself for us. In eternity we will be ever to the glory and praise of God, His unique handiwork, individually and lovingly created.

When the canals and mills were at their peak, when the waterwheels turned and horses pulled the plough and the blacksmith worked at the forge, when potatoes were planted by hand and the thatcher was busy repairing roofs, when the spinning wheel whirled and the hand-loom rattled, the Spirit of the Lord Jesus was alive in this ancient land. His footprints and handiwork were everywhere evident in the lives of simple country people living by faith. The countryside has changed but the Unseen God has not changed and He is alive and changing lives still, forgiving sins, bringing peace and contentment to those who will make Him their all-in-all.

We can be thankful for all our past experiences because they make us the people we are now, each with a unique experience of life, each with a story to tell. And the 'ghosts' are with us still, if only we will look for them, and learn from them.

Reference: (1) 2 Cor.5:17 ESV

44: STEP BACK

I am writing this on the far western coast of Ireland in a quiet hostel hidden under a hill with woods around. It is so quiet you could cut the silence with scissors! Last night, before the Lord led us to this spot to find a roof for the night, we drove along the sea front at Mullaghmore, county Sligo, just a few miles away. At our feet the wild old Atlantic was pounding on the sloping shelves of rock. "Good surfing waves!" our surf-mad son remarked! From where we stood together we could look across the wide reach of Donegal Bay and see the far ranges of the Donegal mountains. Somewhere in that distant vista are some quiet places very familiar to us from previous trips to that area. Over there, in the mist, are the highest sea cliffs in Europe at Slieve League, and beyond that, the quiet bay and the ancient stones associated with St Columba whose name is intricately woven into the name Glencolumbkille.

Behind this hostel is the mighty mountain, Benbulben, almost rising from the sea like a hump-backed whale. There must be many beauty spots hidden in the folds of that memorable rock! And all this can be taken in with a sweep of the eyes, as we stand on that rocky promontory on the edge of this ancient land, cut off from the rest of Europe by mountains and sea, isolated from America by an ocean; a good place to get a perspective on the world as well as on the surrounding countryside. Politics seem insignificant here. God's hand is very evident in the wonders and variety of creation.

We need a place of perspective in our lives, don't we, where we can step back from the norm and take stock of where we are and what is. I had one a few years ago when we lived in Cumbria on the west coast of England, where my work was as a nurse in a hospice for the dying. Daily I travelled the ten miles from home by motorbike to the little town of Ulverston, situated in a fold of the hills on the edge of the Lake District National Park. About a mile outside the town, on Urswick Common, on my way into work, I sometimes used to pull in and pause to look at the view laid out before me. In front, just about visible, I could make out the old house that had been made into a hospice to meet the needs of local people and their families going through the sadness of coping with terminal illness. I knew that in a few short minutes I would be taking off my crash helmet and getting changed into a nurses' uniform and joining my colleagues for another day's work, with all that it might bring in the way of emotional and physical demands.

Each room with its bed would be a world of its own for individuals and their families making their 'journey' though illness and bereavement, and us nurses and team members coming alongside to assist their way a little if possible. For about seven hours my thoughts would be taken up with the practicalities of bathing, dressing, feeding, toileting, dressings, medicines, report writing, drug checking, doctor's rounds, and so many other small pieces that made up the jigsaw of the day, sometimes relieved by a healthy round of laughter with patients and families and fellow-staff members as a necessary relief to the nature of our job.

But from the viewpoint outside town, I could also see beyond that tiny speck that was the hospice, and see laid out the panorama of the Cumbrian mountains running down to the blue sea off the west coast of England. Those mountains were inspiring, immovable, impressive, a continual reminder of the scripture verse found in Psalm 121, verses 1-2: "I will lift up mine eyes unto the mountains: from whence shall my help come? My help cometh from the LORD, which made heaven and earth."

Those mountains formed a backdrop to the town and to the hospice, and in a certain way to everything that would go on that day within the confines of that little building. I would get to work and my eyes would shortly be focused on the immediate and the tasks at hand, and coping with the reality of suffering that could so easily become the over-riding preoccupation of the mind, potentially bringing a state of sadness and depression. God could seem far away in such a place, without faith to see beyond. I knew that it would be comforting and strengthening to go into that day with the vision of those hills and a faith in the God who made them, and to keep all things in perspective.

There is a need to step back and to see the invisible. For only the perspective of the eternal things of God and the realities of heaven can make sense of the confusions and the perplexities of the things of time, with its load of cares that sometimes defy explanation. We all need to step back occasionally and evaluate where we are, and where we are going in life, and what we are doing. When we see it all in a right perspective, then we can get back to the 'grindstone' again, but with an abiding appreciation of a wider world to sustain and calm us.

45: WHAT WILL IT BE?

The Queen was coming to visit Enniskillen, a town in Northern Ireland. It was 12 noon. Crowds had been patiently waiting since 7 a.m., lining the narrow streets of this small country town, hoping at least for a brief glimpse of their monarch. The BBC TV commentator, perched high up on a vantage point, kept the viewers informed as to her progress, as she was a little late, her helicopter delayed by high winds. Police motor cycle outliers were spotted, giving a clue as to her impending arrival and finally a long procession of cars appeared, moving slowly up the main street.

Then, she was here! The excitement amongst the crowds of men and women and children with a day off from school, waving their little flags, was palpable. The cheering reached fever pitch as she stepped out of her chauffeur-driven car, closely followed by her husband, the Duke of Edinburgh. For this was part of Queen Elizabeth's Jubilee year tour, celebrating the sixty years of her reign. And for the population of Enniskillen it was a once in a life-time opportunity not to be missed!

All this for an earthly monarch! As I watched all this on the TV, awaiting treatment in dentist's waiting room a few miles away, "What will it be" I thought, "when the King of Kings appears?" There was a day in His experience when the Lord Jesus Christ did visit a city, Jerusalem, and expectant crowds welcomed him, not with union flags, but with palm branches and shouts of

"Hosanna to the Son of David! Blessed is he who comes in the name of the Lord! Hosanna in the highest!" (1). Too soon, shouts were changed to "crucify, crucify" as Israel's rightful Monarch was despised and rejected of men!

After Jesus finished the work he had been given to do, He returned to His Father's side, where He awaits the day when He will come forth again. And what a day that will be! It's going to be the greatest of all days for the redeemed! We know He is coming; it has been announced. We don't know the day or the time of day. But He won't be delayed. Do you feel the excitement? Are there signs, like outliers, that give an indication that He isn't far away? Are we watching and waiting? Brothers and sisters what will it be when Christ our Saviour and our Lord, appears for us? Amy Carmichael, the Northern Irish poetess, expressed it well:

> What will it be, when, like the wind-blown spray,
> Our spirits rise and fly away, away?
> Oh, lighter than the silvery, airy foam,
> We shall float free. All winds will blow us home.
> We shall forget the garments that we wore;
> We shall not need them anymore.
> We shall put on our immortality,
> And we shall see Thy face, and be like Thee,
> And serve Thee Lord, who hast so much forgiven,
> Serve Thee in holiness - and this is heaven!

Reference: (1) Matt.21:9

46: FLY AWAY HOME

A beautiful spring morning in this part of Northern Ireland! Just time for a breath of air for ten minutes before setting off to attend the Lord's day (Sunday) "Breaking of the Bread" held by the local church of God.

And then, suddenly, walking around the field in front of the house, I heard them! They were high in the sky, heading north. Wild geese! Travelling in a V formation they were no doubt heading for their summer breeding grounds in some remote northern estuary. What freedom; an inspiring sight with a lead bird and other geese following closely behind! They were returning to the land of their nativity, faithfully guided by the created instincts inbuilt into their nature by God.

Fellow Christian, are you looking forward to the day when we also will "fly away home" to be with Christ? A thrilling account comes to mind from a family film that we watched of the same name. Wild geese in Canada had abandoned their nests and eggs as land developers destroyed their habitat. One nest of eggs was rescued by a young girl who accidently came across them. She also had lost her mother in a recent car accident and had not yet come to terms with her loss.

The eggs, placed in a cupboard drawer with a heat lamp, incubated under her watchful attention, and as they hatched they bonded with her, as they would have done with their real mother as they broke out of their shells. Their development continued, following Amy everywhere, until it was time for them to learn to fly and take to the air. This was essential if they were ever to return to the wild and migrate south. However, this posed problems! No amount of cajoling would get them airborne, and they had no 'role model' to teach them and encourage them by example. All the efforts of Amy and her father failed until they hit on the idea of building an engine-powered microlight with wings shaped and painted to look like a wild goose!

Soon the young geese 'clicked' and very obediently, after a few false starts, followed their new 'mother goose' into the air, following the microlight piloted by Amy. Time was getting short and the geese needed to fly south to find winter feeding grounds, or there would be no future for them. But how would they find the way with no adult geese to lead them?

The family hit on an idea! With great enterprise they planned for Amy and her father to fly south in two microlights, leading the geese over the border into north America to an area of wetlands, still wild and undeveloped, where wild geese would be found. What followed was a remarkable journey involving bravery and some near disastrous incidents. At one point, as they crossed the border leading the wild geese in formation, the American air force was scrambled to intercept 'unidentified incoming flying objects' picked up on radar!

Being brought to the attention of the national media resulted in widespread interest in the unique mission to save the geese, with crowds of people watching out on their flight path south. For the last few miles, due to her father having to crash land, the success of the mission rested on Amy's shoulders, as the young girl, with bravery and skill and dedication, led the geese safely to a tumultuous welcome by thousands of well-wishers at the appointed wet-land destination, the geese's winter home! This was a stirring film based on a true story, giving a faint picture of the welcome that awaited our Lord Jesus Christ when He returned triumphant to Heaven His home, after completing His mission on earth. The inspired writer, David, perhaps caught the moment in his Psalm 24:

> Lift up your heads, O gates!
> And be lifted up, O ancient doors,
> That the King of glory may come in.
> Who is this King of glory?
> The LORD, strong and mighty,
> The LORD mighty in battle!
> Lift up your heads, O gates!
> And lift them up, O ancient doors,
> That the king of glory may come in.
> Who is this King of glory?
> The LORD of hosts,
> He is the King of glory!

I returned from my ten-minute break so thankful for the Lord Jesus who took everything on His shoulders to complete His divine mission with absolute commitment to doing His Father's will, providing all who respond to Him with a heavenly home, safe and secure.

What a welcome our 'fore-runner' had when He returned to Heaven (1). And that same welcome will be extended by the Lord Himself to all sinners who have turned to Him, trusted, and followed Him, our glorious leader, on that day when He comes, and we 'fly away home' to be with Him for ever! Now that's a good reason to go to join with fellow disciples this Lord's Day to remember, give thanks and to "sing to the LORD" and to make a "joyful noise to the rock of our salvation!" (2).

References (all Scripture references from the ESV): (1) Heb.6:20 (2) Ps.95:1

47: A String of Blessings

Sadie was in her seventies and my job as a nurse was sometimes to get her up in the morning. Sadie needed help with washing, dressing, using the bathroom and even putting her dentures in. She had her little ritual. When her hearing aid was in place, her hair was brushed, her wrist watch wound, set at the right time and fastened in place, she would always look for one last finishing touch before being wheeled to the dining room for breakfast: 'Put my necklace on, please.'

That necklace! It was a string of pearls, or what looked like pearls, fastened by a delicate gold catch that needed the finest touch to fasten the tiny ring onto a spring clip. And my eyesight and clumsy big hands always struggled with the fastener. When I finally managed to secure the clip, Sadie was happy. And off we'd go to breakfast!

I've thought of my life like that necklace, like a string of bright blessings, coming full circle and fastened with a gold clip. God has carefully threaded on individually created bright blessings as He has worked His sovereign will in my life. Often, as in the experience of the true pearl which forms as the oyster's response to the painful experience of a grit of sand inside the delicate shell, God has allowed hard experiences to be the means of creating the blessings. All done to make us more like Jesus.

"And we know that for those whom love God all things work together for good, for those who are called according to his purpose" (1).

"Blessed...with every spiritual blessing in the heavenly places in Christ" (2).

A string of bright blessings only He could design and put in place. And one day, when they are complete, He will fasten the clip with perfect precision and incomparable timing. All will be finished. And it will be off to a 'supper' in Heaven (3). "Bless the LORD, O my soul, and forget not all His benefits" (4).

References (all Scripture references from the ESV): (1) Rom.8:28 (2) Eph.1:3 (3) Rev.19:7 (4) Ps.103:2

48: DISTANT PEAKS

Like a ring of water bright,
God's blessings lie,
Laid out before our gaze,
We view from mountain high.

Grace, mercy, peace and joy are seen,
God's gifts of love,
And every spiritual blessing given,
Poured out from heaven above.

Goak hill is far too low to see
The distant peaks,
Where eternal blessings hidden lie,
All shrouded yet in mist.

The day will come when clouds disperse,
Our vision clear,
And all transparent to our gaze,
Behold our destination dear.

So let us fix our hope above,
Our compass set,
In joyful expectation wait,
For brighter blessings yet!

SET FREE IN ISRAEL: GILBERT'S STORY

"Shalom." Just recently I retired after working as a nurse for over 30 years in hospitals and hospices in Yorkshire (my birth-place), Cumbria and Northern Ireland. But I wasn't always a male nurse. Once I spent most of my time training to be a craftsman potter with my own workshop. And I didn't always have the peace which I now enjoy. In fact, in November 1975 it was just the opposite; I was in total despair! How did that come about and what changed me?

Born in Yorkshire and in my mid-twenties, I was following my ambition to be a craftsman potter when I became depressed and disillusioned about the state of the world. I felt that it was pointless in continuing to pursue my ambitions. Not knowing what else to do, I found a job on a farm as a general labourer. Another farm worker, knowing my condition, talked to me about the Bible and especially about Jesus Christ coming back again.

Being unsure of my beliefs (despite being brought up to go to church), a chance came to travel to Israel and live there for a year. I set off in January 1975 and once there, lived in Kibbutz Hefzibah in the Jezreel valley in northern Israel. There I also worked on a farm, harvesting grapefruit and cotton, amongst other jobs. I carried with me to Israel a little red Gideon's Bible given to me in 1963 on leaving school. (I still have it!!)

A broken relationship with a Jewish girl that I met in Israel led me into emotional conflict and further despair. Although I read my Gideon's Bible, I didn't understand how to be "saved" from my sins. (I knew my life had been sinful) I was now trying to be a "good" person and even tried to keep all the rules and regulations found in the Bible, including those in the Old Testament (i.e. the law of Moses).

However, I had no peace and one day in November 1975 I found myself at the end of my tether, at breaking point and with no confidence that I was right with God. That day God had mercy on me when at my lowest point (that's often where he meets lost and hopeless people like me!)

Whilst walking through Jerusalem old City and around the Temple site, I suddenly realised that it is not what I needed to do for God that brings peace, but what He has already done for me! I saw in a flash the truth that salvation (i.e. forgiveness and eternal life) is the gift of God, not something to be obtained by good works or keeping rules, but obtained simply through BELIEVING! God shone that light into my heart in His mercy for me!

That moment I was set free from despair! I experienced relief and great peace. Jesus had done everything necessary, had lived a perfect life and offered Himself as a sacrifice for my sins. That day, at the age of twenty-eight, I found hope, purpose in life again, and especially the missing peace!

That experience of being set free in Israel resulted in a sense of great peace, peace which has lasted from then until now, despite times of failure and what are sometimes described as "back-slidings" when old habits, especially sinful ones, have crept in. My peace is made up of three things:

(1) My sins have been forgiven because Jesus died for me, taking the punishment that I deserved. I have been spiritually "born-again." receiving eternal life as a gift from God.

(2) Jesus, the risen Saviour will one day come again for all who have trusted in Him, so there is no need to worry about the future. I am in His Hands.

(3) He has given me His Spirit as a gift to live within me and help me cope with life's worries and anxieties.

Over the years since I returned to England, I married Sue, had a son, and re-trained as a nurse, God has helped me to be a better husband, father and I trust, helped me as a nurse to do my work as well as I can. I know that what He did for me, He can do for you.

*(SHALOM is a Hebrew greeting meaning "peace")

The extended version of Gilbert's testimony is available from www.hayespress.org and is now titled "From Pots to Peace".

MORE TITLES FROM HAYES PRESS

If you've enjoyed reading this book, please consider taking a moment to leave a positive review where you purchased this book! You may be interested to know that Hayes Press (www.hayespress.org) has many more books for you to enjoy. Hayes Press has its own imprint with over a hundred titles available from a wide range of authors. Also, our Search For Truth series by Brian Johnston now stands at almost 50 titles; each contains excellent reading material in a down-to-earth and conversational style, covering a wide range of topics from Bible character studies, theme studies, book studies, apologetics, prophecy, Christian living and more. Our ever-increasing catalogue includes the following titles which you may be especially interested in:

Different Discipleship: Jesus' Sermon on the Mount
A practical, challenging study (complete with questions and prayer prompts) of the "Sermon on the Mount" for followers and would-be followers of Jesus. What makes Jesus and his followers "different"? Find out why this revolutionary, life-changing sermon is why Jesus Christ is regarded as one of the world's most important teachers, even by those who don't follow him as their Lord and Saviour.

Down In My Heart To Stay: Experiencing God's Joy
The children's chorus claims that "I've got the joy, joy, joy, joy

down in my heart ... down in my heart to stay!" but many Christians often don't experience this as a reality in their everyday lives. This is vitally important because it not only means we miss out on what God wants for us, but it can damage the effectiveness of our witness for Jesus Christ at the same time. Filled with contributions from a range of authors, this very practical book:
- explores what Biblical joy really is
- reminds us what we can be joyful about as Christians
- highlights some of the things that can rob us of our joy
- outlines what is needed to maintain our joy or restore it when it is lost.

Hope For Humanity: God's Fix for a Broken World

Daily headlines remind us that this world is broken in so many different ways; an honest look within ourselves reveals deep problems there as well. This book pinpoints the same cause behind both and rejects all man-made solutions in favour of the divine one – the sending of His Son at Bethlehem on a mission that would lead to a cross at Calvary – with a challenge to every reader to accept or reject it.

A very conversational book, full of anecdotes and illustrations, yet direct and challenging - ideal to share with someone you know who you wish to reach with the good news of Jesus Christ, or to strengthen and sharpen your own faith in the gospel.

Light From Darke Box Set: 200+ Devotionals

This set comprises three volumes of Bible-based thoughts from Reg Darke, with 230 encouraging, challenging and informative mini-messages that mature and new believers will appreciate alike.

More Like Jesus: Six Goals For Godliness
The goal of every Christian is to be more like Jesus - but what does that look like? In this short book, Phil Capewell sets out 6 attributes that characterized Jesus' life and encourages us all to be like Him: compassion, gentleness, humility, long-suffering, patience and love.

Pure Milk: Nurturing New Life in Jesus
Whether you're looking to help a new Christian on the discipleship path or are a new believer yourself, you'll benefit from this concise mentoring guide by Search For Truth's Brian Johnston, which walks through 8 key areas for early spiritual development, including the importance of a relationship with Jesus, the role of the Holy Spirit, learning to talk with God, and how to walk victoriously as a disciple.

What Have We To Give? (Volumes 1 & 2): Bible Devotions From A Missionary To Burma
Alan Toms was a missionary who devoted many years of his life to missionary work in Burma (now Myanmar) and who was also known for his devotional writing, much of which centred around the person of the Lord Jesus Christ and the encouragement of his disciples. Also available separately, Volume 1 contains a brief background to his life and work and 65 of his short devotional thoughts. Volume 2 contains a further 73 thoughts. Rather like "Chicken Soup For The Soul", each volume is ideal to be read in one sitting or as part of daily Bible reading and devotional times.

ABOUT HAYES PRESS

Hayes Press (www.hayespress.org) is a registered charity in the United Kingdom, whose primary mission is to disseminate the Word of God, primarily through literature. It is one of the largest distributors of gospel tracts and leaflets in the United Kingdom, with over 100 titles and hundreds of thousands dispatched annually. Hayes Press also publishes Plus Eagles Wings, a fun and educational Bible magazine for children, six times a year and Golden Bells, a popular daily Bible reading calendar in wall or desk formats. Also available are over 100 Bibles in many different versions, shapes and sizes, Christmas cards, Christian jewellery, Eikos Bible Art, Bible text posters and much more!

www.ingramcontent.com/pod-product-compliance
Lightning Source LLC
Chambersburg PA
CBHW071506040426
42444CB00008B/1515